DYLAN THOMAS'S
WALES

DYLAN THOMAS'S
WALES

HILARY LAURIE

WEIDENFELD & NICOLSON
LONDON

CONTENTS

PROLOGUE

Dylan Thomas – his name alone releases a stream of associations and meanings. Acclaimed poet from a nation of poets and singers, brilliant talker and story teller, famous bon viveur, the standard bearer for twentieth-century Welshness and Wales – so we think of him now. But his identity and his destiny were more ambiguous and more complex than this.

'ONE; I AM a Welshman; two: I am a drunkard; three: I am a lover of the human race, especially of women,' he is said to have told the audience at one of the very popular poetry readings which he gave in the last years of his life. He knew that this was what they expected, what they wanted to hear, but he was more or less speaking the truth. He was without doubt a drinker, if not a drunkard; women, especially his wife, and the care and support women gave, were vital to him. And his Welsh identity was very important too, although it was not always something he could fully or comfortably embrace. He would parade it when it suited him, but he could as easily dismiss it: 'Land of my fathers. My fathers can keep it.'

As a young man he was determined to escape from the provincialism of Swansea. He did not see himself, person or poet, as belonging to a specifically Welsh tradition, and he was puzzled later when people remarked on the Welshness of his poetry. 'I've never understood this racial talk...' Yet he conceded that if he had been born and brought up anywhere else he would have been extremely unlikely to have become a writer.

His parents were Welsh-speaking, with strong ties to Welsh culture and customs, but they spoke only English with their children and, like their neighbours in the Swansea suburb of Uplands, their home was middle-class and Anglo-Welsh. D.J. Thomas admitted to one of his son's friends that Dylan wasn't much of a Welshman, a view shared by a good number of his fellow countrymen. Dylan could take a jocular view of his position: '...non Welsh-speaking, non-rationalist, non-degreed, non-chapel going, and not to be trusted...' Others viewed him more harshly. With a number of fine Welsh writers writing in English, he has been judged incomplete, incapable – since outside the Welsh language – of expressing the true soul of Wales.

Dylan Thomas's chief subject was himself; he wrote about little else. His themes are nostalgia, the search for lost innocence, and the relationship between life, creativity and death. He wrote mostly of himself as a boy or young man: the places, sights and sounds of his past became the metaphors and emblems of his writing. The trees and birds, sea and rocks of the south Wales countryside are a part of his voice. Wales is the landscape of his imagination.

But Wales both enriched and enraged him. Isolated in a small provincial town, he was forced to explore and examine his own life. Such a small community was the ideal place for him: in London and elsewhere he lost his way. It is no accident that his best work was done in Swansea, New Quay and Laugharne. But small towns made him feel trapped and he could not live in them for long. His adult life was a series of restless movements between Wales, London and, in his last years, America.

Home was for Dylan Thomas what it is for most of us – a place we have to leave, a place we take for granted but from which we draw

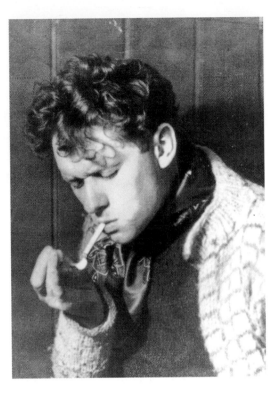

Dylan sent this photo of himself to his friend and fellow poet Vernon Watkins in 1938. 'Why I want you to think of me...as a tough, I don't know.'

energy and support. At the end of a radio talk, 'Living in Wales', which he gave in 1949, he debated whether he was the same man in London as he was in Wales. 'Lost and blown about in London town, a barrel-shaped leaf, am I still the same, I said to myself, as that safe and sound loller at the corner of Wales who, to my memory, was happy as a sandman.' The answer to his question proved elusive, but no less important for being so. 'I know', he said, 'that I am home again because I feel just as I felt when I was not at home, only more so.'

CHAPTER 1

Young and Easy

'I first saw the light of day in a Glamorgan villa, and, amid the terrors of the Welsh accent and the smoke of the tinplate stacks, grew up to be a sweet baby, a precocious child, a rebellious boy, and a morbid youth.'

So WROTE DYLAN THOMAS, aged nineteen, to his first girlfriend. Sketching his life to date in 'a touching autobiography in one paragraph', he wanted to amuse and impress her. He had been born on 27 October 1914 in the best bedroom of 5 Cwmdonkin Drive, Swansea, a brand-new semi-detached house into which his parents had moved in the summer of the same year. They were delighted with their baby son: their daughter, Nancy, was eight years old, and earlier babies had not survived. There was some dispute between them over what to call him, but his father got his way. He chose Dylan, then a little-used name, after the 'fine boy-child with yellow hair' who makes a brief appearance in the Welsh medieval romances *The Mabinogion*, and Marlais, the bardic name of the nineteenth-century preacher-poet Gwilym Marles, the baby's great-uncle. These were powerful and distinctive names for a little child who, his mother felt, although healthy enough, was not very robust.

Dylan would grow up knowing no Welsh, so it is unlikely that these links with the past meant a great deal to him, but for his father, D.J. Thomas, they had certain significance. His uncle Gwilym Marles had been a famous man in his time, both poet and active in

5 Cwmdonkin Drive, Swansea, the 'Glamorgan villa' which was Dylan's birthplace and childhood home

ABOVE *'The Poplars', Johnstown, Carmarthen, once the home of Dylan's father's parents, now a pub*
RIGHT *'Suburbia set at an impossible angle' – the view down Cwmdonkin Drive across Swansea and the bay*

local politics and in the Unitarian church. D.J. Thomas was someone for whom literature was all-important; it would be a strong point of contact between him and his son. He was a complex and difficult man. Born in 1876 in Johnstown, then a village outside the town of Carmarthen, the son of a railwayman, he won a scholarship to the university at Aberystwyth where he got a first-class degree in English. But from then on things

Dylan as a little boy. This photograph belonged to his mother.

did not go as he had wished. He wanted to be a poet and, failing in this, he felt that he deserved to get a university post. He achieved neither of these, and he was to spend all but two years of his working life teaching English to the boys of Swansea Grammar School, which he considered poor compensation for the loss of what might have been.

His marriage, too, was something of a compromise. His wife, Florence, was very different in both character and interests. She had been born in Swansea, on the poorer, eastern side of the town – her father was a railway porter, later promoted to inspector – but her family retained strong links with their relatives in the countryside. She was one of seven children, and her brothers and sisters, Dylan's aunts and uncles, were important figures in his childhood. Unlike his taciturn, withdrawn father, his mother was loving, sociable and garrulous. He allowed her to indulge and spoil him as a child; when adolescent he was less tolerant of her, but later they rediscovered a strong, shared affection.

Home, the 'Glamorgan villa', was in Uplands, a new, expanding suburb of Swansea. It was the first house Dylan's parents owned and it represented a definite step up for them. D.J. Thomas may have felt that schoolmastering was beneath him, but at least he could now present himself as a home-owning, middle-class, professional man.

Uplands was a pleasant place to live, with substantial houses, in terraces or semi-detached, set among trees and gardens on a steep hillside overlooking the town and Swansea Bay. It has been affectionately described as 'suburbia set at an impossible angle'; it was a genteel, respectable neighbourhood governed by strict religious codes, where drink was frowned on and sexual immorality unthinkable.

Swansea had a prosperous air at the time of Dylan's birth in 1914. The munitions industry, answering the needs of the First World War, masked the dangerous decline in coal exports and the gradual withering of industry in south-west Wales. By the 1930s there would be mass unemployment and great poverty. Uplands and west Swansea were

*Centre stage, Dylan poses in a Swansea photographer's
studio with his mother, sister Nancy and a family friend.*

Swansea, 'the most romantic town I know', seen from Mumbles across Swansea Bay.

much less affected by this than the poorer districts in the east of the town or the mining villages in the valleys to the north. Uplands offered shops, churches, chapels, a hotel and cinema, and the new university college was not far away. Florence Thomas had a maid to help her in the house, as well as someone who came in to wash the family's clothes, but sometimes money was in short supply and she had to borrow from her family and stagger payment of the household bills.

Dylan's friend Wynford Vaughan-Thomas thought of Swansea between the two world wars as an 'unplanned, smokily romantic town'. The proximity of the coalfields of south Glamorgan had brought the copper industry to the town, and often a plume of smoke hung over the hills. In the centre, chapels, pubs, banks, drapers' shops and cafés stood haphazardly side by side. The town hall was tucked away in the docks, the museum tangled up in railway arches; the art gallery's nearest neighbour was a working-men's club. German bombing in the Second World War would change the town beyond recognition. Until that time, for Dylan Thomas it was 'the most romantic town I know...an ugly, lovely town...crawling, sprawling, slummed, unplanned, jerry-villa'ed, and smug-suburbed by the side of a long and splendid-curving shore'.

Swansea people are rarely out of sight of

In Dylan's childhood around two-thirds of the people in Swansea spoke only English. He could claim to have grown up 'amid the terrors of the Welsh accent', but the words he heard were mostly English ones. His parents were Welsh speakers, and when his mother's relatives came to visit, or were visited in their turn, he heard Welsh spoken. But this met with strong disapproval from his father. He had decided that he and his wife would not pass the language on to their children. His colleagues and his neighbours in Uplands probably did the same. Indeed, so determined were the Thomases that their children would not be socially at a disadvantage, that Nancy and Dylan went to elocution lessons, which gave Dylan what he called his 'cut-glass' English accent, but happily did not in any way lessen the richness and resonance of his voice.

the sea or the hills. The town sits on the wide curve of Swansea Bay, once generously compared by the poet Walter Savage Landor to the Bay of Naples. The tidal range is exceptional and, at the ebb, the bay is a vast expanse of sand. To the east, across the River Tawe which divides the town, are the port and docks; to the west the shore slips away towards Mumbles Head and the Gower Peninsula beyond. From the town centre the streets rise steeply to meet a ring of hills behind, creating a natural boundary, a sense of containment, even of isolation. Swansea is in its own special way a border town – the meeting place of land and sea, of the northern mining valleys with rural Wales to the west, of two languages, English and Welsh.

Later, when he was working as a cub reporter on the *South Wales Evening Post*, Dylan would get to know more of his home town – the river, the docks, the Strand and the more disreputable districts where coal trucks rumbled over railway arches, sailors drifted from pub to pub and the air held a faint promise of illicit sex. While he was still a boy, his world was in the western suburbs, particularly Cwmdonkin Drive on the 'swathed hill stepping out of town'. The Thomases' home was one of three pairs of

The view from 5 Cwmdonkin Drive across the town and bay towards the Mumbles and the Gower

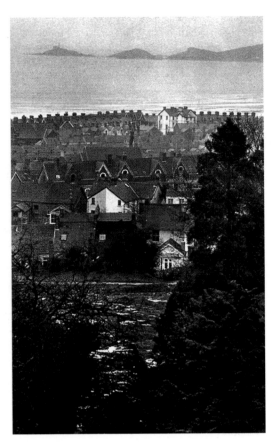

houses in a very steep road, opposite a park. The house was narrow, but deep from front to back. Overlooking the small front garden was the parlour, used only on Sundays and on special occasions – a visit from the preacher, or by family or friends from England, or by mourners at a funeral, all hesitant and uncomfortable on the unused chairs, beneath the framed needlepoint texts and two solitary china dogs. Behind the front parlour was a middle room, D.J. Thomas's den, his book-lined 'brown study' where his young son would soon sit reading and writing. And further back were the breakfast room and kitchen, his wife's demesne. There she would cook and bake and sew, or sit drinking tea and chatting with family and women friends. Home from school, D.J. Thomas would retreat at once into his own room where, if the weather was cold, his wife would have lit the gas fire and left out his carpet slippers.

From the bedrooms upstairs it was possible to look down over the town towards the docks and the bay towards Mumbles and the Gower. Dylan's room, his 'bedroom by the boiler', was small and rather dark, shared with the hot-water tank whose rumblings punctuated his thoughts and kept him company. In his late teens, by which time he was reading widely and writing poetry, he pinned pictures of writers on his walls –

Shakespeare, Robert Browning, Walter de la Mare, Rupert Brooke, and on the mirror he pasted a copy of a poem which had appeared under his name in a local newspaper. 'I was always waiting for the opportunity to bring someone into my bedroom – "Come into my den; excuse the untidiness; take a chair. No! Not that one, it's broken!" – and force him to see the poem accidentally. "I put it there to make me blush." But nobody ever came in except my mother.'

It was not at first sight an exciting neighbourhood for a lively young boy; the 'morbid youth' would find it press hard upon him. But for the young child there

Cwmdonkin Park, Swansea

Cwmdonkin Park photographed in 1910. The park was Dylan's first playground – 'a world within the world of the sea-town'.

were worlds within worlds to discover and explore. First of all the front garden and whatever lay immediately outside the door; then the park, across Cwmdonkin Drive, a few minutes' walk away, 'itself a world within the world of the sea-town...so near that on summer evenings I could listen, in my bed, to the voices of other children playing ball on the sloping, paper-littered bank; the Park was full of terrors and treasures.' He was taken there for the first time in his pram when he was only a few days old; it was to become a vital reference point, fixed in his memory and in his imagination for the rest of his life.

In one of his early poems (reworked before it was first published in 1941), he remembers the trees, the lake, the drinking fountain with its chained cup, the park keeper collecting leaves, the children playing, and, on the edge of their carefree games, the sinister, solitary figure of a hunchback.

The hunchback in the park
A solitary mister
Propped between trees and water
From the opening of the garden lock
That lets the trees and water enter
Until the Sunday sombre bell at dark

Eating bread from a newspaper
Drinking water from the chained cup
That the children filled with gravel
In the fountain basin where I sailed my ship
Slept at night in a dog kennel
But nobody chained him up.

Like the park birds he came early
Like the water he sat down
And Mister they called Hey mister
The truant boys from the town
Running when he had heard them clearly
On out of sound

Past lake and rockery
Laughing when he shook his pape
Hunchbacked in mockery
Through the loud zoo of the willow groves
Dodging the park keeper
With his stick that picked up leaves.

And the old dog sleeper
Alone between nurses and swans
While the boys among willows
Made the tigers jump out of their eyes
To roar on the rockery stones
And the groves were blue with sailors

Made all day until bell time
A woman figure without fault
Straight as a young elm
Straight and tall from his crooked bones
That she might stand in the night
After the locks and the chains

All night in the unmade park
After the railings and shrubberies
The birds the grass the trees the lake
And the wild boys innocent as strawberries
Had followed the hunchback
To his kennel in the dark.

The drinking fountain in Cwmdonkin Park

The experiences and sensations of Dylan's childhood reappear in his writing throughout his life, sometimes only hinted at in fleeting images of happiness or innocence, of *temps perdu*, or fully and openly explored, as in his story 'Patricia, Edith, and Arnold', the funny and touching tale of two young women confronting their two-timing suitor

RIGHT *Mirador Crescent, Swansea, where Dylan attended Mrs Hole's nursery school*
BELOW *Memorial to Dylan in Cwmdonkin Park with the closing lines of his poem 'Fern Hill'*

Oh as I was young and easy in the mercy of his means
time held me green and dying
though I sang in my chains like the sea

DYLAN THOMAS

in Cwmdonkin Park. The park was a very important part of his growing up. At first, running free up and down banks and through trees, playing cowboys and Indians, sailing boats on the lake; later, feeling the first stirrings of interest in girls and poetry, it was a place which set his imagination free and where he could observe the world and begin to position himself in it.

Dylan's mother, convinced that he was not very strong, kept him at home until the age of seven. When at last he went to a small nursery school in nearby Mirador Crescent, he was used to getting his own way. Mrs Hole ran the school in her house with her red-faced husband and her daughter who would take the little boy on her knee and indulge him in her turn. He was a precocious child, imaginative and mischievous, with a cherubic face, wondering eyes and a head of blonde curls. When the children misbehaved, Dylan usually managed to escape blame. No one, teachers or children, wanted to cross the ever-watchful Mrs Thomas. In

her eyes Dylan could do no wrong, even when he highjacked the school play with his antics, running around the stage brandishing a walking stick and spraying the audience with orange peel. Whatever he learned at Mrs Hole's school, years later he recalled only the smell of rubber boots, the sound of piano lessons drifting down from upstairs, the rough and tumble and pranks played. After school the children would make their way home up the hill along a small lane, bragging and boasting, concocting stories about themselves and their families, sharing secrets. This memory stimulated Dylan's adult fancy in his first radio broadcast, 'Reminiscences of Childhood'. Eager to have a secret to share, he tells his friends that he can fly.

And when they do not believe me, I flap my arms and slowly leave the ground, only a few inches at first, then gaining air until I fly waving my cap level with the upper windows of the school, peering in until the mistress at the piano screams and the metronome falls to the ground and stops, and there is no more time. And I fly over the trees and chimneys of my town, over the dockyards, skimming the masts and funnels, over Inkerman Street, Sebastapol Street, over the trees of the everlasting park, where a brass band shakes the leaves and sends them showering down on to the nurses and the children, the cripples and the idlers, and the gardeners, and the shouting boys, over the yellow seashore and the stone-chasing dogs and the old men and the singing sea.

The memories of childhood have no order and no end.

Dylan was getting to know more of the world outside 5 Cwmdonkin Drive and, at the same time, he grew more aware of his family and his life at home. The gap of eight years between him and his sister Nancy made it difficult for them to feel close. She features very little in his memories and his writing. A sensitive, observant child, he cannot have failed to notice the great differences between his parents. It is hard to understand why they married; perhaps it was not purely a matter of choice. Florence Thomas would say in later years that they met at a fair in Johnstown. At that time she was working as a seamstress in a drapery shop in Swansea; D.J. Thomas was already a teacher. They married fairly quickly, in 1903, perhaps because she was pregnant, but there is no record of a baby's birth before Nancy's in 1906. For the first years of their marriage they lived in Sketty on the western outskirts of Swansea, but before Nancy was born they moved closer to the centre of town, apparently in response to Florence Thomas's fears for the child's health, for in Sketty there was as yet no proper drainage. If indeed she lost her first baby, this would explain why she was so protective of Nancy and Dylan. As it turned out, he was much less sickly than she thought, but he had very brittle bones – 'chicken bones', she would call them, and many falls throughout his life meant a succession of broken arms and ribs. He also had a weak chest, which was not helped by his very heavy cigarette smoking, a habit he started at the age of fifteen at school. He was exempted from military service in 1940 because of his bad lungs, by which time he had a violent smoker's cough.

Florence liked to kiss and cuddle her children, and Dylan grew used to her devoted caring for him when he was thought to be ill. What was at first a lazy pleasure grew into a dangerous need; he would learn to allow other people to do things for him and lose the ability or wish to look after himself. But being forced to stay in bed brought benefits. His mother would read to him when she had time, or she would give him comics to look at by himself. It was with these, she said, that he taught himself to read. His father's approach was very different: he read Shakespeare to his young son. Dylan may not have understood what he heard, but he would have been aware of the pleasure his father took in the words, and of the power and

resonance of his voice. D.J. Thomas's pupils at Swansea Grammar School had little cause to remember him warmly, but they never forgot his readings from Shakespeare, which made them see that there was something in the plays for them. His reading to Dylan, before the little boy could himself speak, was his way of introducing him to the colour, shape and sound of language. D.J. Thomas had failed to become a poet; he hoped, he intended his son would succeed where he had failed.

Dylan's mother soon realized that the only way to keep her son happy at home was to give him pencil and paper. With these he would disappear into his bedroom and write poems. Often in need of a subject, he asked his sister for help. On one occasion, ether in fun or because she could not be bothered to give the matter much thought, she suggested that he write about the kitchen sink; another time she suggested an onion. His father encouraged Dylan to read and write, but he seems to have written nothing himself. He chose instead to sit alone with his thoughts over a drink. He did not drink at home; instead it became his habit to go to a local bar in the evening, under the guise of taking a walk. No one was deceived, but it was never openly admitted or discussed. Florence Thomas would keep up the pretence that he never touched alcohol. Caitlin, Dylan's wife,

The Church of Paraclete in Mumbles where Dylan went as a child
to hear his uncle, the Rev. David Rees, a very powerful preacher

was enraged by this hypocrisy, by the need to keep up appearances. D.J. Thomas was a grumpy man who kept himself to himself, who hated guests and was happiest by himself in his room. Acutely conscious of his thinning hair, he took to wearing a hat both inside and outside the house. He was sarcastic, quick-tempered, a man held in awe by everyone who knew him. Dylan would describe him as a militant atheist, whose atheism was not based on the non-existence of God but on a violent personal dislike of him. On rainy days he would growl, 'It's raining, blast Him!'; when the sun shone he would retort, 'The sun is shining – Lord, what foolishness!' His pessimism deepened as he aged and his health failed. As he neared death, Dylan wrote how 'the world that was the colour of tar to him is now a darker place'.

Consciously or unconsciously, his family must have had to develop strategies for living with him. Fortunately Florence was a member of a big family, and she remained close to her three brothers and three sisters. Her sister Annie had married a farmer, Jack Jones, and together they farmed Fernhill, a key place in Dylan's childhood pantheon which he commemorated in his most famous poem. Her sister Dosie married a preacher; Florence would take Dylan to his chapel in Newton to the west of Swansea,

where he became familiar with the Bible's stories and with its rhythms and cadences which echo and sing in Dylan's own poems. His mother did not lose her links with the people and countryside of her childhood and youth. Her family and friends visited her in Swansea, and Dylan was sent to stay with them, to eat fresh food and breathe clean country air. Stories in his *Portrait of the Artist as a Young Dog*, his 'adolescent auto-biography', tell of such visits, of the world he discovered outside the town, on a farm or in a small village. In 'A Visit to Grandpa's' the young boy, staying with his grandfather for the first time, finds himself with someone for whom events in the mind are more real than life lived in the present. He calls out 'Whoa!' and 'Gee-up!' in the night; his bed has become a horse-drawn cart and he is the driver. Convinced he will soon die, he dresses himself in his best clothes and heads for Llangadock, determined not to be buried at Llanstephan where you cannot 'twitch your legs without putting them in the sea'. His friends go in search of him and gently bring him home. The little boy observes, listens, only half understands. This is a familiar place and these are familiar people, but he realizes he does not really know them at all.

In the autumn of 1925, just weeks before his eleventh birthday, Dylan started at Swansea Grammar School. He had grown

LEFT *Dylan aged eleven, winner of the mile race on sports day at Swansea Grammar School*

RIGHT *Dylan and his school friends took the tram 'that shook like a jelly' to the Mumbles to watch the fishermen and clamber among the cast-iron struts of the pier.*

during his four years at nursery school, but he was still slightly built, with curly hair and large soft lips and eyes. Luckily there was within him a hidden toughness, for he now found himself in a much bigger, and less predictable world. Swansea Grammar was a fee-paying school, full of the sons of the middle class, and where his own father had taught for the best part of twenty years. It would not have taken him long to discover that his father was as much his own man here as he was at home, held in awe not for his abilities but for his bad temper and ferocious tongue. He was the master in charge of the school magazine, and his permission was needed before anything was accepted for publication. Dylan wasted no time in submitting material and, in his first term, had a comic poem published.

Perhaps encouraged by this success, he sold a poem to the *Western Mail* in Cardiff. 'His Requiem' was published in the paper in January 1927, and for over forty years it was assumed to be by Dylan Thomas. It has since been identified as the work of another writer. This deception has been taken as proof of how very much Dylan wanted to be a poet, how desperately he wanted to prove himself and satisfy his father's aims and ambitions for him. It is possible that there is another explanation, that the poem was sent in error. All his life Dylan copied out poems he liked and wanted to understand fully. He did this as a young boy, and he continued it when he was an established poet himself and planning readings of other poets' work alongside his own. Many such copies exist among his papers.

He continued to send poems to other papers and to the school magazine. Along

The Pier, The Mumbles. Swansea

with some success on the running track and in the school dramatic society, this was more or less his only contribution to school life. He was a very half-hearted student. This may have been in part a reaction to his position of master's son, or it may have been his way of coping with the larger, harsher world of which he was now a part. If he could not easily be first, he would be last; rather than struggle to get results, he would fail spectacularly. The one subject he cared about, and in which he excelled, was English. In 'Return Journey', the radio broadcast in which he describes a return visit to Swansea in June 1947, he remembered the kind of boy he then was:

...he looked like most boys, no better, brighter or more respectful; he cribbed, mitched, spilt ink, rattled his desk and garbled his lessons with the worst of them; he could smudge, hedge, smirk, wriggle, wince, whimper, blarney, badger, blush, deceive, stammer, improvise, assume offended dignity or righteous indignation as though to the manner born; sullenly and reluctantly he drilled, for some small crime, under Sergeant Bird, so wittily

RIGHT *Mumbles Head and Bracelet Bay*
OVERLEAF *Decorative tiles on a wall at Mumbles*

nicknamed Oiseau, on Wednesday half-holidays, appeared regularly in detention classes, hid in the cloakroom during algebra, was, when a newcomer, thrown into the bushes of the Lower Playground by bigger boys, and threw newcomers into the bushes of the Lower Playground when he was a bigger boy; he scuffled at prayers, he interpolated, smugly, the time-honoured wrong irreverent words into the morning hymns, he helped to damage the headmaster's rhubarb, was thirty-third in trigonometry, and, as might be expected, edited the School Magazine.

Dylan was protected from the other masters by his father's being one of them and by their fear of him. Throughout the whole school, discipline was light or, as one of the boys described it, 'civilized and relaxed'. Pupils who did not want to work were not forced to do so. Daniel Jones, Dylan's closest friend, tells the story of how the two of them set out to miss a French lesson, but were seen by the headmaster as they passed his study on their way to town. When he asked where they were going, Dylan replied, 'We're going to play billiards. Any objection?', to which the headmaster replied, 'Oh, you wicked boys. I hope you get caught.'

The teachers must have held out little hope of Dylan achieving very much, and it

'Warmley', Eversleigh Road, home of Dylan's school friend Dan Jones, within walking
distance of Cwmdonkin Drive 'through solid, deserted, professional avenues lined with trees'
OVERLEAF Langland Bay. Dylan would take 'medicinal walks' along the cliffs, in breaks
from writing and reading.

cannot have been easy for D.J. Thomas to accept that any expectation he had of his son going to university would have to be abandoned. At first sight he appeared rebellious, unteachable, aimless. One of his school friends remembered him in his last year burning holes in the prefects' room floor with a hot poker, and Dylan described himself how he would hang about the town, dawdling among the railway arches, mooching along the shore, idly watching the tankers and cargo boats leave the docks and set out to sea. He went with his friends to Saturday matinées at the cinema in Uplands. They played cricket, of a kind, on the cindery surface of the Recreation Ground, or took the open tram 'that shook like a jelly' to Mumbles pier, to watch the fishermen sit over their rods at the end, or to hang upside down from the cast-iron struts underneath. On Sunday nights, after chapel, they would make for the promenade and whistle at girls.

But not all his friendships were so hedonistic or his days so aimless and carefree. One of his first and most enduring relationships was with Daniel Jones. Dylan describes how they first met in 'The Fight', a story which sizzles with the life and energy they shared. A motiveless punch-up in a school playground led to the discovery of a boy with talents and interests equal to his own, and together they created a private world of poetry, music, word games and outlandish fun. Dan Jones was the first of his contemporaries with whom Dylan could exchange ideas, who took his poetry seriously and understood what he was trying to do. He was an exceptionally gifted boy: it is said that by the age of twelve he had written several novels and could play both the piano and violin. He would go on to write symphonies and other classical pieces, and he learned eight languages fluently. Jones's home, 'Warmley', some ten minutes' walk from Cwmdonkin Drive, would become a second home for Dylan in his late adolescence. There he found books by the major writers of the day, complementing the reading to which he had been guided by his father. During the early years of their friendship, Dylan made huge progress as a writer, discovering his voice and laying the foundations of his style which was to change very little over the years, writing or drafting in notebooks a very large proportion of his best poems.

Much of the enjoyment and richness of their relationship lay in its playfulness and inventiveness. They made music together, Dan on the piano, Dylan pretending to play the violin. They performed impromptu chamber music by resident composer Dr Percy (Dan) on saucepan lids and Woolworth's whistles, which was answered by loud bangs on the party wall by the

neighbours next door. They wrote poems together, sometimes writing alternate lines. They played word games, planned to produce a magazine; they set up their own broadcasting station, Warmley Broadcasting Company, using loudspeakers to relay programmes from one room to another. Together they plotted rebellion and revenge on smug, sanctimonious Swansea. They little knew then what Dylan would discover later, that they needed the safety and security of Swansea as much as they needed to escape from it. In the summer of 1935, alone (briefly) in Ireland, he wrote to remind his old friend, then living in London, of their private Warmley world and its importance for their poems and music.

I never thought that localities meant so much, nor the genius of places, nor anything like that. I thought that the soul went round like a Gladstone bag, never caring a damn for any particular station-rack or hotel-cloakroom; that gestures and genius made the same gestures in Cockett and Cockfosters...We must, when our affairs are settled...go back to Uplands or Sketty and found there, for good and for all, a permanent colony; living there until we are old gentlemen, with occasional visits to London and Paris, we shall lead the lives of small-town anti-society, and

entertain any of the other members of the WARMDANDYLANLEY-WORLD who happen to visit the town.

For the present, they were completely absorbed in what they were doing. Dylan's story 'The Fight' ends with the boys about to part for the night. They run into the street, glancing back at deeply depressed Mrs Bevan, a neighbour and family friend, watching them from an upstair's window, her face pressed hard against the glass. They both hope and fear that she may jump.

At the corner Dan said: 'I must leave you now, I've got to finish a string trio to-night.'
'I'm working on a long poem', I said, 'about the princes of Wales and wizards and everybody.'
We both went home to bed.

Doubtless Dylan was working on a poem, probably not a long one and certainly not one about figures from Welsh history. From April 1930 until the end of 1934, between the ages of fifteen and nineteen, he wrote 200 poems at least, storing them in a series of notebooks, school exercise books kept for the purpose. Four of these have survived, but there were others. Dylan at one point refers to ten. These notebook poems are the fair

The church at Brechfa, Carmarthenshire, home of Dylan's father's family in the 1830s

copies he made from innumerable drafts and reworkings done on scraps of paper, written on both sides, 'often upside down and criss cross ways, unpunctuated, surrounded by drawings of lamp posts and boiled eggs, and in a very dirty mess'. By this point he had abandoned rhyme: the first notebook, begun in April 1930, is headed 'Mainly Free Verse Poems'. Dylan's subjects are love, girls, sex, death, the meaning of life – common adolescent preoccupations. But these are not common adolescent poems, heartfelt outpourings of emotion. They are carefully worked, the poems of a very alert young man who is closely focused on what he is doing.

In these four years, 1930 to 1934, Dylan wrote four times as much poetry as in the remaining nineteen years of his life. He was writing in the dark, for himself alone. Apart from Dan Jones and one or two other friends with whom he shared them, the poems remained in the notebooks, unpublished and unseen. What he was now producing no longer suited the school magazine or the other journals he knew, but it would not stay hidden for very long. Eventually, he would print thirteen poems from these notebooks in his first book, *18 Poems*, and three further collections, *25 Poems*, *The Map of Love* and *Deaths and Entrances*, include poems first witten in these years. This was a time of ferocious and fertile activity.

It is possible that his growing sense of himself and of his vocation made him less interested in what he was supposed to be doing at school, or Dylan may have taken his poetry more seriously because he was achieving so little in class. Whatever the cause and effect, he left Swansea Grammar School at the end of the school year, in July 1931, aged sixteen and a half. He promised his mother that one day he would be as good a poet as Keats. He saw Keats as a role model – the poet who burned brightly and died young. Dan Jones saw more in him of Arthur Rimbaud – and nicknamed Dylan 'the Rimbaud of Cwmdonkin Drive' – a truant from the French provinces, brief years of intense productivity, a short, rebellious existence, he was an unlikely model for a happy life.

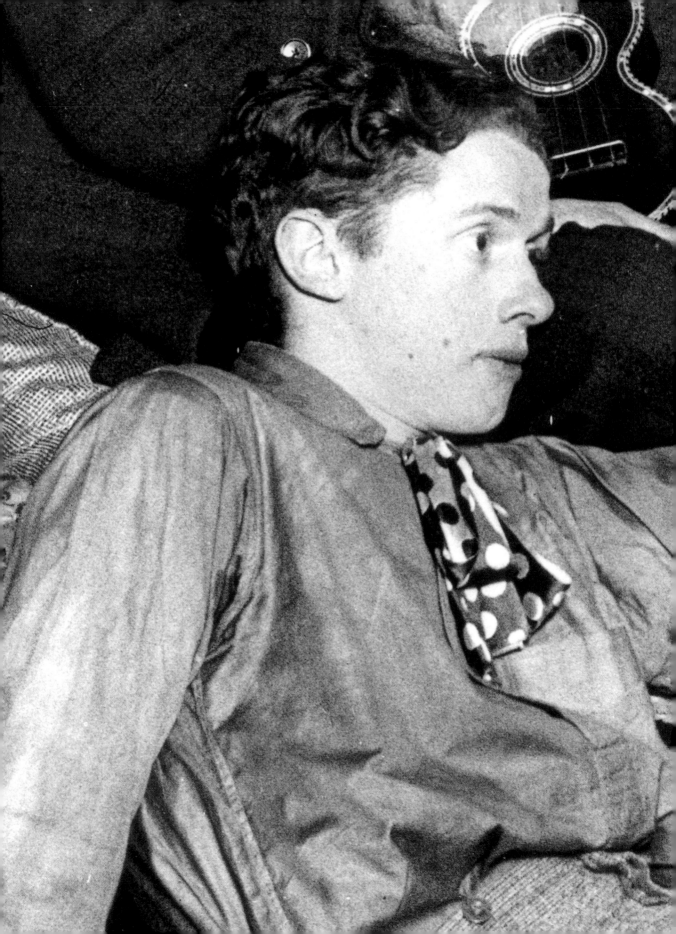

CHAPTER 2

Beast, Angel, Madman

'He'd be about seventeen or eighteen...and about medium height. About medium height for Wales, I mean, he's five foot six and a half. Thick blubber lips; snub nose; curly mouse-brown hair; one front tooth broken after playing a game called Cats and Dogs in the Mermaid, Mumbles; speaks rather fancy; truculent; plausible; a bit of a shower-off; plus-fours and no breakfast, you know...a bombastic adolescent provincial bohemian with a thick-knotted artist's tie made out of his sister's scarf, she never knew where it had gone, and a cricket-shirt dyed bottle-green; a gabbing, ambitious, mock-tough, pretentious young man; and mole-y, too.'

SOME FIFTEEN YEARS on, this was how Dylan Thomas characterized himself as a young reporter, but it is not how he seemed in the summer of 1931 when he first appeared in the offices of the *South Wales Daily Post*. His new colleagues met a reserved young man, very well turned out, who said little and applied himself to the job at hand. He knew that he was very lucky to have a job at all – these were very depressed times and young men much better qualified than he was were without work. But the abrupt transition from schoolboy to employee was not easy, and the poems he was writing in his notebook at the time suggest painful heart-searching and some unhappiness. On the other hand, as a reporter he learned a lot about the world around him, absorbing information and impressions which would resurface in his writing later. He set about

Dylan, the young actor; in the early 1930s he was a member of the Little Theatre Company, Mumbles.

refashioning himself, burying the rebellious schoolboy and discovering the raffish young man. Soon his loud clothes, tall stories, chain smoking and love of beer clearly signalled his distance from respectable Swansea, that 'blowsy town on the furthest peaks of the literary world'.

Dylan started in the *Post*'s printing department, reading out proofed copy so that it could be checked and corrected. After two months or so he moved on to become a junior reporter, but he soon lost interest in the routine visits to fire stations, hospitals, mortuaries and court hearings in search of news, and he was tempted to file reports on events he had not attended, at the same time failing to report news which he had allowed to pass him by. He much preferred to spend time with his friends in the Kardomah café, drinking coffee and 'arguing the toss' about 'music and poetry and painting and politics, Einstein and Epstein, Stravinsky and Greta Garbo, death and religion, Picasso and girls'. Eventually it was suggested to him that he would be better off elsewhere and, less than eighteen months after starting work, he was without a job. He may have felt a little ashamed of his sacking; he pretended to his friend Trevor Hughes that he had been offered a five-year contract which he had refused, fearing the 'slow stamping out of individuality, the gradual contentment of

life as it was, so much per week, so much for this, for that, and so much left over for drink and cigarettes. That was no loife for such as Oi!'

His plan was to work as a freelance journalist, contributing to the *Post* and to a sister paper, the *Herald of Wales,* and this at first he did. He also wrote more and more poetry, and within a few weeks, in February 1933, he started a new notebook. Conditions for work seemed ideal, 'in my little ivory temple, immune from the winds and whips of the world, shut, if you like, Proustlike in my conservatory'. But there are hints that all was not well.

Ears in the turrets hear
Hands grumble on the door,
Eyes in the gables see
The fingers at the locks.
Shall I unbolt or stay
Alone to the day I die,
Unseen by stranger-eyes,
In this white house?
Hands, hold you poison or grapes?

His bedroom was his sanctuary, but the currents and storms of family life surged and raged on the other side of his door. The ivory tower he had constructed for himself was not without cost to others: it required his mother's care and devotion, and provoked his sister's rage. Both Nancy and Dylan were now at home, neither with a regular job. She strongly resented the fact that the life of the household seemed to be organized around him, that he was allowed to do pretty much what he wanted because he was 'a writer'. Their mother devotedly cooked, fetched and carried for him; he felt free to take money from his sister's purse and borrow her clothes. She could not even write to her boyfriend (soon to be her husband) when she wanted to, for Dylan had first rights to the family ink bottle. They managed to get on rather better on stage, at the Little Theatre, Mumbles where they were both members of the company, a lively young group of amateur actors seen as somewhat advanced by certain sections of Swansea society, performing a range of plays from Restoration dramas to light comedies by Noel Coward.

'My speciality', claimed Dylan, 'is the playing of madmen, neurotics, nasty "modern" young men and low comedians – quite straight acting.' By all accounts he was a good actor, but he was to end up by being dismissed from his role as leading man in a play called *Martine* because during the dress rehearsal he went too often to the bar when he was not needed on stage. There were frequent arguments at home too about his drinking.

His days in 5 Cwmdonkin Park followed a regular routine:

At half past nine there is a slight stirring in the Thomas body, an eyelid quivers, a limb trembles. At a quarter to ten, or thereabouts, breakfast, consisting of an apple, an orange, and a banana, is brought to the side of the bed and left there along with the Daily Telegraph. Some five minutes later the body raises itself, looks blindly around it, and, stretching out a weak arm, lifts the apple to its mouth. Waking is achieved between bites, and...the webs of the last night dreams are remembered and disentangled. Then...the banana is peeled and the newspaper opened...The orange, incidentally, is never touched until I get downstairs, the process of peeling and pipping being too cold and lengthy for such an hour of the morning. When the reports of rapes, frauds and murders have been thoroughly digested, I light a cigarette, very slowly lay my head back on the pillow, and then, without any warning, leap suddenly out of bed, tear off my pyjamas, scramble into a vest and trousers and run, as if the fiends of winter were at my heels, into the bathroom...And then downstairs where, after another cigarette, I seat myself in front of the fire and commence to read, to read anything that is near,

41

Arthur's Stone on Cefn Bryn, Gower, a prehistoric monument familiar to Dylan from his walks alone and with friends.

poetry or prose, translations out of the Greek or the Film Pictorial, a new novel from Smith's, a new book of criticism, or an old favourite like Grimm or George Herbert, anything in the world so long as it is printed...Then down the hill...for one (or perhaps two) pints of beer in the Uplands Hotel, before going back home to lunch. After lunch, I retire again to the fire where perhaps I shall read all the afternoon – and read a great deal of everything, or continue on a poem or a story I have left unfinished, or to start another or to start drafting another...or to type something already completed, or merely to write – to write anything, just to let the words and ideas, the half remembered half forgotten images, tumble on the sheets of paper. Or perhaps I go out, & spend the afternoon in walking alone over the very desolate Gower cliffs, communing with the cold and the quietness. I call this taking my devils for an airing. This takes me to tea-time. After tea, I read or write again, as haphazardly as before, until six o'clock. I then go to Mumbles...First I call at the Marine, then the Antelope, and then the Mermaid. If there is a rehearsal I leave these at eight o'clock and find my way to the Little Theatre, conveniently situated between the Mermaid and the Antelope. If there is no rehearsal, I continue to commune with

Gravestone of Ann Jones, Dylan's aunt, at Llanybri, near her home at Fernhill.
Her death in 1932 was the inspiration for Dylan's poem 'After the funeral'.

these two legendary creatures, and, more often than not, I conduct metaphysical arguments with a Chestertonian toper... Then a three mile walk home to supper and perhaps more reading, to bed and certainly more writing. Thus drifts an average day. Not a very British day. Too much thinkin', too much talkin', too much alcohol.

This was written to amuse, but the reader has to marvel none the less at Dylan's self-absorption, at his father's tolerance and his mother's devotion. Yet, had he managed to get the grades which would have taken him to university, Dylan's life as a student would probably have been little different from the one he was currently leading. He was getting up rather late as many students would, doing nothing for anyone in the family but himself, and he was probably drinking too much, but he was reading voraciously and he was writing a great deal. In fact, these years in Swansea, between the time he left school in the summer of 1931 and his departure for London at the end of 1934, would prove to be the most important and productive of his writing life.

This is not to say that he was completely happy with his lot, at one with the world in which he found himself. On 1 March 1933 he copied a poem into his notebook which began:

I have longed to move away
From the hissing of the spent lie;
And the old terrors' continual cry
Growing more terrible as the day
Goes over the hill into the deep sea,
Night, careful of topography,
Climbs over the coal-tips where children
    play;
And the repetition of salutes
For ladies, the stale acts of the mutes;
And the thunder far off but not far enough
Of friendship turned to ghosts' hates
By telephone calls or notes,
For there are ghosts in the air
And ghostly echoes on paper;
I have longed to move but am afraid.

He began sending out poems to editors in London. Geoffrey Grigson at *New Verse* sent them back; A.R. Orage at the *New English Weekly* did not. In the late spring of 1933, with 'And death shall have no dominion', Dylan made his first appearance in a London magazine. When he made his first trip to London in August, to visit his sister and her husband on their houseboat on the Thames, he went to see several editors and explored possible outlets for his work. With Nancy gone, things should have been even easier for him at home, but in August 1933 his father was discovered to have cancer of the mouth. Months of successful treatment

Worm's Head, Gower Peninsula, 'a rock at the world's end', which Dylan found both exhilarating and frightening

followed – he was to live for a further twenty years or more – but Dylan was frightened and troubled. He was fascinated by death, but he preferred to deny the existence of illness. This one was too close to be ignored. He couldn't dismiss it as he had done the death from cancer of his aunt Ann Jones a few months before. Then he had remained detached, even though he knew that she had loved him, and that he had been happy with her during childhood holidays on her farm, Fernhill. In the version of his poem 'After the funeral' which he drafted three days after she was buried he took a very jaded view of her death and its mourning, and in a letter written at the time he admitted that he had no interest in reaching out to other people. 'I don't feel worried, or hardly ever, about other people. It's self, self, all the time. I'm rarely interested in other people's emotions, except those of my pasteboard characters. I prefer...style to life, my own reactions to emotions rather than the emotions them-selves.' In January 1934, when his father was well enough to go back to work, he told a friend that he had not been overwhelmed by worry during the illness, for he had been protected by 'my self-centredness, my islandic egotism which allows few of the day's waves to touch it...I become a greater introvert day by day...'

W.B. Yeats famously remarked that a poet

BELOW *High Street, Swansea, later changed beyond recognition by wartime bombing. In his story*
'Old Garbo' Dylan recalls his 'dead youth in the vanished High Street nights'.
RIGHT *The home and shop of Dylan's friend and political mentor Bert Trick, in Glanbrydan Avenue*

'is never the bundle of accident and incoherence who sits down to breakfast'. This is very true of Dylan Thomas. Frequently he seemed at odds with himself; his inner life, the life he lived in his head was often quite unlike his life in the everyday world. As he grew older this gap between the private and the public man would widen with tragic consequences. At the age of nineteen, it was still only a curiosity, something he enjoyed exaggerating for effect. At this point he had no real difficulty balancing single-minded absorption in his own self and feelings with empathy for others and a lively, expanding social life and circle. Many of the friends with whom he had sat putting the world to rights in the Kardomah café moved away from Swansea, but new friends filled their places. One was Bert Trick –

Dylan would refer to him as 'my communist grocer' – a socialist and Marxist who lived above his shop in Glanbrydan Avenue, down the hill about ten minutes' walk from Cwmdonkin Drive. Bert Trick was very well read and wrote poems himself, and soon Dylan was going regularly with friends to his house for music and readings and talk. Mrs Trick's sandwiches, jelly and blancmange were an added attraction – Dylan had a ruinously sweet tooth. Her husband, as well as providing a listening ear and kindly advice, worked to widen Dylan's knowledge and understanding of society. In Glanbrydan Avenue Dylan mounted a 'soapbox of bright colours', from which he displayed 'grand, destructive arguments learned so industriously and vehemently from you on winter evenings after

Cwmdonkin sonnets and Lux to sweet ladies – you gave my rebelliousness a direction...' But Dylan's rebellions were always more social than political. Unlike his contemporaries in the 1930s who were writing poetry that was engaged and politically aware, he chose the world of symbol and dream, not that of social and political struggle. He was to be a visionary rather than a polemical or discursive writer. Yet Bert Trick later testified to Dylan's powers of empathy and compassion at this time. Trick did not think of him as a heartless young man, a view supported by another very close friend Trevor Hughes, who was struck too by

his maturity of mind. Not yet twenty-one years old, he had already identified the person he wanted to be; he had a strong sense of his role and place in the world.

He made an important breakthrough when one of his poems, 'That sanity be kept I sit at open windows', was accepted by the *Sunday Referee* for its 'Poets' Corner'. This was not a poem he specially valued, he never reprinted it, but it introduced him to his first real girl-friend and led to the publication of his first book. When she read it in the *Sunday Referee*, the young poet Pamela Hansford Johnson decided to write to Dylan, so beginning what

'The Rimbaud of Cwmdonkin Drive' – Dylan aged 19, photographed
when he was staying with Pamela Hansford Johnson in London

he termed 'the dazzling correspondence of two diverse but well attuned imaginations'. They were not to meet until February of the following year, 1934, and then only briefly, but they wrote to each other often and at length until the end of the year when he moved to London, by which time they had fallen in love and come to think that they might marry. She had also begun to realize, sadly, how great would be the risks and cost to herself if they did. Dylan's letters to her are a wonderful record of these Swansea years, and of the energy and growth in and behind his early writing.

Her letters meant a great deal to him. Quite soon he felt that he knew her as well as he had known anyone in his life, and that he was able to be completely honest with her. This was to be his undoing: she loved the young poet who wrote her funny, affectionate letters, helped her with her own writing, shared with her his ambitions and ideals, but she was afraid of his extremes, of his mood swings, his need for drink and his sexual adventurousness.

In his letters to Pamela, Dylan both observed and invented himself. He was writing to someone outside Wales, someone whom he had never met, who admired him and his work. His appearance, his ambitions, his family, Swansea, Wales – all could be edited, dramatized, alchemized.

Don't expect too much of me. (It's conceit to suppose that you would); I'm an odd little person. Don't imagine the great jawed writer brooding over his latest masterpiece in the oak study, but a thin, curly little person, smoking too many cigarettes, with a crocked lung, and writing his vague verses in the back room of a provincial villa.

But he was quick to tell her that he was greater than his surroundings, that they were stifling him and that he had to make his escape. Living in Swansea might have something to be said for it, but life in the Welsh countryside was unbearable.

I am staying, as you see, in a country cottage, eight miles from a town and a hundred miles from anyone to whom I can speak to on any subjects but the prospect of rain and the quickest way to snare rabbits. It is raining as I write, a thin, purposeless rain hiding the long miles of desolate fields and scattered farmhouses. I can smell the river and hear the beastly little brook that goes gurgle-gurgle past this room. I am facing an uncomfortable fire, a row of china dogs, and a bureau bearing the photograph of myself aged seven – thick-lipped, Fauntleroy-haired, wide-eyed, and empty as the bureau itself.

The road between Blaen Cwm and Llanstephan. Dylan's mother's family had strong links with this part of Carmarthenshire.

There are a few books on the floor beside me – an anthology of poetry from Jonson to Dryden, the prose of Donne, a Psychology of Insanity. There are a few books in the case behind me – a Bible, From Jest To Earnest, a History of Welsh Castles. Some hours ago a man came into the kitchen, opened the bag he was carrying, and dropped the riddled bodies of eight rabbits on the floor...

It is impossible to tell you how much I want to get out of it all, out of narrowness and dirtiness, out of the eternal ugliness of the Welsh people, and all that belongs to them, out of the pettiness of a mother I don't care for and the giggling batch of relatives. What are you doing? I'm writing. Writing? You're always writing. What do you know? You're too young to write... And I will get out. In some months I will be living in London. I shall have to get out soon or there will be no need. I'm sick, and this bloody country's killing me.

Such a sense of alienation was painful, but the isolation in which Dylan was writing was not necessarily damaging or inhibiting. Because he was so much on his own – well away from London, in Wales, in a provincial town, writing in the privacy of his note-books, he was able to take risks with language and ideas. He was free of fashion

The beach at Rhossili, at the tip of the Gower Peninsula, scene of the camping expedition in Dylan's story 'Extraordinary Little Cough'

and orthodoxy; there was nothing or no one to stifle his very individual voice. It is very possible that his self-pitying rage against the land of his birth was as much a clearing of lungs, a flexing of muscles, as a genuine *cri de coeur*, and that he was using Wales as a necessary irritant, something which provoked him to write.

At other times he could be more generous.

I often go down in the mornings to the furthest point of Gower – the village of Rhossili – and stay there until evening. The bay is the wildest, bleakest and barrennest I know – four or five miles of yellow coldness going away into the distance of the sea. And the Worm, a seaworm of rock pointing into the channel is the very promontory of depression. Nothing lives on it but gulls and rats, the millionth generation of the winged and tailed families that screamed in the air and ran through the grass when the first sea thudded on the Rhossili beach…

One day when I know you even better than I do now, you must come & stay with me, sometime in the summer. Swansea is a dingy hell, and my mother is a vulgar humbug; but I am not so bad, and Gower is as beautiful as anywhere.

There is one bay almost too lovely to look at. You shall come and see it with me; we shall both utter words of maudlin wonder, and swoon away on the blasted heath.

By the beginning of 1934, after two-and-a-half years of living and working at home, he began to talk seriously about moving away. He felt that he had to earn some money. In his present circumstances he could not begin to think of marrying and, more significantly, even though his father had returned to work he was not the man he had been, and he and his wife were beginning to discuss selling the house in Cwmdonkin Drive and moving to the country outside Swansea where other members of their families lived. In fact they did not do this for another two years, but the end of Dylan's comfortable way of life was in sight. He toyed with the idea of working in a publisher's office or joining 'a bad repertory company in Coventry, or some place like that'. Perhaps he could go to Russia with a Welsh Communist organization. He enjoyed fantasizing but failed to follow through. Instead he talked about compiling an anthology of prose and poems by contemporary Welshmen, and he continued to send his poems to magazines in London. Several editors had expressed cautious interest in his work – one had made the startling accusation that fecundity such as Dylan's could

only be the result of automatic writing – but although they felt they could not ignore the poems, they could not like them. 'And so we go on, meeting nothing but courtesy and interest, nothing but a rather bewildered refusal to print.'

Many found his ideas and his imagery rather shocking; most found his poems difficult and obscure. His own father regretted his son did not write poems he could understand. But Dylan held his ground. His stated aim as an artist was 'to prove beyond doubt to myself that the flesh that covers me is the flesh that covers the sun, that the blood in my lungs is the blood that goes up and down a tree'. What he wanted to say was inseparable from the metaphors and symbols which expressed it. 'Through my small, bonebound island I have learnt all I know, experienced all, and sensed all. All I write is inseparable from the island. As much as possible, therefore, I employ the scenery of the island to describe the scenery of my thoughts, the earthquakes of the body to describe the earthquakes of the heart.'

But his failure to get work published was dispiriting and in the spring of 1934 it brought him close to despair. From April onwards he did not add any poems to his notebooks.

The old fertile days are gone, and now a poem is the hardest and most thankless act of creation...It gives me now a physical pain to write poetry. I feel all my muscles contract as I drag out from the whirlpooling words around my everlasting ideas of the importance of death on the living, some connected words that will explain how the starry system of the dead is seen, ordered as in the grave's sky, along the orbit of a fruit or a flower. But when the words do come, I pick them so thoroughly of their live associations that only the death in the words remains. ...I shall never be understood. I think I shall send no more poetry away, but write stories alone.

But success was just around the corner. One of his poems was chosen for the Book Prize awarded from time to time to a contributor to the *Sunday Referee*'s Poet's Corner. (Pamela Hansford Johnson was the first winner of this particular prize, Dylan the second.) This meant not simply recognition, it also brought the promise of book publication. This was the breakthrough Dylan so badly wanted and needed.

The prize-winning poem, a fusion of the poet with his images and his ideas, brilliantly embodied Dylan's credo.

The force that through the green fuse drives the
   flower
Drives my green age; that blasts the roots of trees
Is my destroyer.
And I am dumb to tell the crooked rose
My youth is bent through the same wintry fever.

The force that drives the water through the rocks
Drives my red blood; that dries the mouthing
   streams
Turns mine to wax.
And I am dumb to mouth unto my veins
How at the mountain stream the same mouth
   sucks.

The hand that whirls the water in the pool
Stirs the quicksand; that ropes the blowing wind
Hauls my shroud sail.
And I am dumb to tell the hanging man
How of my clay is made the hangman's lime.

The lips of time leech to the fountain head;
Love drips and gathers, but the fallen blood
Shall calm her sores.
And I am dumb to tell a weather's wind
How time has ticked a heaven round the stars.

And I am dumb to tell the lover's tomb
How at my sheet goes the same crooked worm.

Dylan and Pamela met for the first time in February 1934 in London, both very nervous. He had come with a ready-prepared phrase – 'Have you seen the Gauguins?' – to break the ice. They were very quickly at ease with each other. They went together to the theatre, ballet, a concert, and they spent a lot of time walking on Clapham Common near where she lived in Battersea with her mother. Or they sat in pubs talking and reading each other's work. He was keen to arouse her maternal and protective instincts; he would emphasize his smallness (although she was not tall herself), his poor health, his low

*Portrait of Dylan by his Swansea friend Alfred Janes. They
shared a room when Dylan first moved to London in late 1934.*

weight. Pamela, in response, acted in what he described as a 'vaguely sardonic secretarial capacity'. He recognized how straight and traditional she was and, for the moment, this appealed to him. Always, one part of him craved order and a regulated life while another side of him regularly sabotaged it. Beast, angel, madman – Caitlin was very aware of these contradictions, but he could never agree with her, a true bohemian, that he had not completely shed the values of his early background. But to Pamela he was happy to admit, 'You alone know how True-Blue I really am, & what a collection of old school ties my vest conceals.'

In March 1934 Dylan wrote to Pamela telling her that he loved her: What was she to do? 'Oh it is so difficult to reply.' By early May he was warming to his theme.

I believe with all my heart that we will live together one day as happily as two lobsters in a saucepan, two bugs on a muscle, one smile, though never to vanish, on the Cheshire face. But I will never exhaust my flow of pessimism, for, sadistically, it gives me a delight, or a pain and a delight mixed in one, to imagine the most dreadful things happening to us, to imagine a long future of bewilderment and disillusion ending in Tax Collectors...matchselling and sterile periods of the production of cracker-rhymes that we, in our hopeless megalomania, will imagine as the disregarded fruits of genius. That one day you will vomit at the sight of my face, and I at the tones of your voice.

Worse was to come some three weeks later – a letter scrawled in pencil, probably with little foundation in truth, confessing to a four-day drinking session and sexual dalliance with the fiancée of a friend. Was Dylan asking her for help by acknowledging that he was drinking too much and was not in control of himself? Or was he giving free rein to the little boy in him, doing and taking what he wanted whatever the consequences, certain that he will be forgiven afterwards? Pamela forgave eventually, but her confidence in him was permanently damaged.

Perhaps he hoped that it might help if she were to see him on his home ground, in safe, stable Swansea. He wrote to persuade her to pay a visit, giving her a thumbnail sketch of what she would find:

G.W.R station. Shabby, badly built streets. Unutterable melancholy blowing along the tramlines. Quarter of an hour's tram ride up a long, treed road. A square, a handful of shops, a pub. Up a treed hill, field on one side, houses on the other. Near the top of the hill a small, not very well painted,

Dylan's mother, Florence Thomas, at the tea table in 5 Cwmdonkin Drive in the early 1930s

gateless house. Large room, smaller room, study, kitchen. Private school in field opposite. Nice field. Tennis court above. Very nice, very respectable. Not much traffic. Lot of sparrows. My own room is a tiny renovated bedroom, all papers and books, cigarette ends, hardly any light. Very tiny. I really have to go out to turn round. Cut atmosphere with book-knife. No red cushion. No cushion at all. Hard chair. Smelly. Painful. Hot water pipes very near. Gurgle all the time. Nearly go mad. Nice view of wall through window. Pretty park nearby. Sea half a mile off. Better sea four or five miles off. Lunatic asylum mile off. Workhouse half a mile off. All this sounds depressing, but you must come down. And come down soon, as soon as you can. If it's hot and summery, we can have a wonderful time. And if it rains, we can fug all day and all night with the greatest pleasure in the world.

Gwilym Marles Thomas, poet, priest, politician, Dylan's great-uncle and namesake

Pamela and her mother came to Swansea in September. They stayed in the Mermaid Hotel, which offered them some protection from Mrs Thomas's ceaseless chatter, but it was not enough to save the visit. The weather was awful, so that escape into the countryside was impossible. Pamela discovered that Dylan was younger than she thought – he was still only nineteen, with no financial prospects of any sort. She resorted to hysterics and soon left for London, now knowing for certain that he was very unlikely ever to be her husband. Their relationship did not survive his move to London a few weeks later. Within two years she married someone else. Dylan would marry Caitlin shortly afterwards.

He began to make plans for his move to London. He was eager to be off. A visit to Caradoc Evans in Aberystwyth confirmed his view of the Welsh as intolerant of great writers. Evans had outraged the Welsh establishment with his collection of satiric short stories, *My People*, published in 1915. He gave Dylan and his friend Glyn Jones a warm welcome. After tea and conversation, the two young men toured the pubs, 'drinking to the eternal damnation of the Almighty & soon-to-be-hoped-for destruction of the tin Bethels. The university students love Caradoc, & pelt him with stones whenever he goes out.' Dylan's final literary engage-ment in Swansea was equally against the grain. Asked to speak to the local literary society, he chose pornography and the nineteenth-century novel as his topic, one of little immediate relevance to his audience of some thirty-five women 'of a dim, uncertain age, most of them virgins, & all with some smattering of Freud & Lawrence'.

Accompanied by 'communist grocer' Bert Trick, becomingly clad in red (he liked to think) and holding a silver-topped walking stick, he proceeded to shock his audience into a stunned silence. It did not help that Bert Trick's boots were covered in mud, and that they had been to the pub beforehand.

Dylan had to leave Wales in order to understand what it meant to him. For the moment nothing Welsh pleased him, not even Laugharne which he visited in early summer with Glyn Jones. It was certainly 'the strangest town in Wales', but he did not warm to it, perhaps because Jones disapproved of his drinking, and it was 'a hopeless, fallen angel of a day', with a 'hell-mouthed mist blowing'. On the sands of the estuary a small group of men and women were gathering cockles, hundreds of oyster catchers circling round them. The women scraped at the sand with the handles of broken jugs, then washed the shells they had collected in nearby rock pools. Dylan found it impossible to reconcile the literary

qualities of the scene before him with the brutishness of the people in it, with the crudeness and hopelessness of their lives, the women

sweating the oil of life out of the pores of their stupid bodies, and sweating away what brains they had so that their children might eat, be married and ravished, conceive in their wombs that are stamped with the herring, &, themselves, bring up another race of thick hipped fools to sweat their strength away on these unutterably deadly sands.

His sights were set on London, on his girl-friend, on the literary world. Sitting by the side of the estuary at Laugharne, he took in every detail of his surroundings – the scarlet ants crawling out from under the rocks, the broken masts of a stranded ship in the distance, the tiny fish in the cold rock pools. But he was not in tune with his surroundings. He wanted to observe, to feel, to experience life in his own way, on his own terms.

Thus armed, he set out for London to celebrate the publication of his first book of poems.

O make me a mask and a wall to shut from your spies
Of the sharp, enamelled eyes and the spectacled claws
Rape and rebellion in the nurseries of my face,
Gag from a dumbstruck tree to block from bare enemies
The bayonet tongue in this undefended prayerpiece,
The present mouth, and the sweetly blown trumpet of lies,
Shaped in old armour and oak the countenance of a dunce
To shield the glistening brain and blunt the examiners,
And a tear-stained widower grief drooped from the lashes
To veil belladonna and let the dry eyes perceive
Others betray the lamenting lies of their losses
By the curve of the nude mouth or the laugh up the sleeve.

The young poet – Dylan in the late 1930s

CHAPTER 3

The Map of Love

'Before the internal-combustion engine, before the invention of the wheel, oh what a long time ago, in the Golden Days…Do you remember them, Fred? The Golden Days, in London, when we were exiled bohemian boily boys. There were three of us then: you and me and Mervyn Levy, three very young monsters green and brimming from Swansea, stiff with lyrics and ambition and still-lives, all living together in big, bare barmy beautiful room kept by a Mrs Parsnip, as far as I can remember, in Redcliffe Gardens…And here I am nostalgically mourning those dead green salad days, and that very conventional period of anti-conventionality, just as we used to mourn, in this Parsnip's mousey-and-cabbage palace, the town we had left behind us for ever and ever. For ever and ever.'

SO DYLAN THOMAS reminisced in the last year of his life. He had left Swansea for London almost twenty years earlier, in November 1934, to live in a house off the Fulham Road with two young men from Swansea, both painters. He shared a room with Alfred Janes; his old schoolfriend Mervyn Levy had the room above. Both were to remain his close friends. Dylan's 'Swansea gang' was very important to him, one of the things which drew him back again and again to Wales, but it played little part in his life elsewhere. He liked to keep his several worlds distinct and separate. The 'bohemian boily boy' newly arrived from the provinces wanted a free hand, for London was full of

Dylan around the time of his marriage in 1937

new people and exciting new possibilities.

Those salad days looked rather better across the years than they were at the time. Even then Dylan had his doubts. He told Bert Trick back in Swansea how he was living in a quarter of pseudo-artists who gave 'the most boring Bohemian parties I have ever thought possible', where 'slightly drunk, slightly dirty, slightly wicked, slightly crazed we repeat our platitudes on Gauguin and Van Gogh as though they were the most original things in the world'. But he claimed he was managing to meet interesting people outside this circle – Henry Moore, Wyndham Lewis, Nina Hamnet, as well as a notorious artist's model and dabbler in black magic, Betty May, who, he liked to think, would pay him in kind for a piece of ghost writing he was to do for her.

But none of this was helping his own writing. The muddle and mess of his and Janes's room made it difficult for him to concentrate. 'For yards around me I can see nothing but poems, poems, poems, butter, eggs and mashed potatoes mashed among my stories and Janes's canvases. One day we will have to wash up, and then, perhaps, I can really begin to work.' Nor was it good for his health; he could not tolerate such a ragged life for long. By Christmas, some six weeks after he had left, he was back in Swansea, recovering from the excesses of talk, dirt, beer and bad food. This was to become a pattern. He rarely stayed away from Wales for long. He would confidently set out, burn the candle at both ends, then retreat back home for rest and recuperation. At the end of 1934 he was able to bring with him early copies of his first book, *18 Poems*. The first print run was modest, only 250 copies, and he would have to wait some time for reviews, but Dylan was justified in thinking that, at the age of only twenty, he had made his mark.

Mrs Thomas worried about her son when he was away from home; she relied on the more sober and serious Fred Janes to look after him. But, in London again in early 1935, he continued to live life to the full, and soon he would be one of the most familiar and most sought-after figures in the pubs and clubs of Soho and Fitzrovia. But no amount of drink and company could resolve the conflict in him between the excitements of city life and what he called his 'nostalgia of open and grassy spaces'. He was beginning to place more importance of his surroundings. 'I do really need hills around me before I can do my best with either stories or poems; the world here is so flat and unpunctuated...' Yet once again in Swansea, he found things very dull. His friends were at work during the day and, in any case, their interests and his were no longer always in tune. When he heard that the novelist Richard Hughes, living not far away in the Castle House in Laugharne, had expressed admiration for his poetry, he arranged to call on him. And he found another new friend in the poet Vernon Watkins who had written to him after reading *18 Poems*. When they first met in the spring of 1935 Watkins found a young man,

slight, shorter than I had expected, shy, rather flushed and eager in manner, deep-voiced, restless, humorous, with large, wondering, yet acutely intelligent eyes, gold curls, snub nose, and the face of a cherub. I quickly realized when we went for a walk on the cliffs that this cherub took nothing for granted. In thought and words he was anarchic, challenging, with the certainty of that instinct which knows its own freshly discovered truth...

They began to meet regularly at the Kardomah café during Watkins's lunchbreaks from his work in a Swansea bank, or at his house at Pennard on the Gower, or in Cwmdonkin Drive. They read and discussed their poems, and Dylan would read out the stories he was writing. Vernon Watkins soon became one of his most important and loyal readers and critics. Dylan greatly respected his opinion, although he seems not to have greatly liked his poetry. It lacked what his own verse so abundantly possessed – 'the

strong, inevitable pulling that makes a poem an event, a happening, an action perhaps, not a still-life, or an experience put down, placed, regulated.'

Watkins was one of several new friends disarmed by Dylan's intelligence, fluency and charm who were willing to put themselves out and help him in return for his friendship. He had the knack of making people feel that they must look after him. So he found himself staying with a young history lecturer, Alan Taylor, and his wife Margaret in their cottage in the Peak District. A.J.P. Taylor would soon call him a shameless sponger, but his wife grew increasingly obsessed with Dylan, treating him and his family with great generosity, to the detriment of her own finances and marriage. From Cheshire he moved to Ireland to stay with the poet Geoffrey Grigson in an isolated artist's studio 'perched on a field on a hill facing a lot of wild Atlantic' near Glencolumbkille, west of Galway. Grigson returned to London, leaving Dylan alone in rainswept countryside which he liked to think was haunted by the spirits of the dead and damned. He was working well but, unhappy with the prospect of being on his own for some weeks, he began to feel homesick for Swansea. Yet he knew that there he would be little better off. 'I wouldn't be at home if I were at home. Everywhere I find myself seems to be nothing but a resting place between places that become resting places in themselves. This is an essential state of being, an abstraction as concrete as a horsefly that's always worrying the back of your neck.'

The only solution seemed to be to shuttle to and fro between Wales and London, from his mother's care and attention in Cwmdonkin Drive to the fun-loving and frenzied crowds in the pubs and bars around Charlotte Street. The more his drinking companions enjoyed his company, the more he seemed to need their admiration and attention. His stories and antics grew wilder and more outrageous. His friends were dismayed by his chameleon-like ability to go with the flow, to suit his mood to that of present company. Drinker, raconteur, sexual adventurer, he returned home at the end of 1935 not only exhausted but probably suffering from some sexually transmitted disease which would require a fairly lengthy recuperation. His mother would say years later that he had had some sort of breakdown at this time. Whatever the problem, it was a rather chastened young man who celebrated his twenty-first birthday with his parents in October 1935.

For some months he had been working on the poems which he hoped would make his second book, but negotiations with Richard Church, poetry editor at publishers J.M.

Dent, were lengthy and vexed. Church found his poetry too complex and often incomprehensible, but he sensed its power and, in spite of himself, finally agreed to bring out *25 Poems* in late 1936. Several reviewers too would complain of obscurity; one remarked that Dylan seemed not to know at this point which way to turn, an astute observation for now he was unsure of himself and of his vocation. The great surge of energy which had carried him forward through his schooldays and his apprentice-ship seemed to be on the wane. Words and images now came to him with such diffi-culty, demanded so much effort from him, that they seemed to him still-born. He was to write very little poetry during 1936 and 1937. Not until he was once again settled in one place, first in Hampshire and then Wales (this time in Laugharne), would he begin to work fluently and productively once again.

But first there was to be a fundamental change in his life. In the spring of 1936 he met Caitlin Macnamara who would become his wife. They met for the first time in a London pub, the Wheatsheaf in Rathbone Place, introduced by the painter Augustus John who was a friend of Caitlin's mother and, reputedly, Caitlin's first lover. (She would protest that this was demanded by John of all his female sitters, a simple assertion of his prowess and power.) Dylan

*Caitlin photographed with Augustus John in 1955 after Dylan's death. John
was a friend of her mother and had been, it was said, Caitlin's first lover.*

The Gorsedd stones at Fishguard. Dylan, Caitlin and Augustus John came here to the National Eisteddfod in 1936.

boasted that he was in bed with Caitlin ten minutes after he first set eyes on her. Her less dramatic version of events is the more likely: she confirmed that they had an affair and spent several nights and days at the nearby Eiffel Tower Hotel at Augustus John's expense, after which she returned to her mother's house in Hampshire and Dylan went off to Cornwall to stay with yet another caring friend, Wyn Henderson, who felt it was her turn to look after him. At this point neither he nor Caitlin seemed to regret that they had parted so quickly and after such a brief acquaintance. He worked on some short stories, and he toyed with the idea of a book on Wales, part fiction, part auto-biography, part travelogue. Other friends were staying in the neighbourhood; he got into bed with his hostess, and he began a relationship with another woman nearby. But he was not content. As ever, he felt that he would be better off somewhere else.

> I'm not a country man; I stand for, if anything, the aspidistra, the provincial drive, the morning cafe, the evening pub ...man made his house to keep the world and the weather out, making his own weathery world inside; that's the trouble with the country: there's too much public world between private ones.

The Castle House and 'the clock of sweet Laugharne, the clock that tells the time backwards, so that soon, you walk through the town, from Brown's to the gulls on the strand, in the only Golden Age!'

He went back to Swansea in the early summer and shortly afterwards he and Caitlin met for the second time. Fred Janes, who had a painting in a competition in Fishguard, home that year to the National Eisteddfod, suggested to Dylan that they go together to the judging which was to be presided over by Augustus John. Dylan arranged that on the way they would have lunch with Richard and Frances Hughes at the Castle House in Laugharne where both John and Caitlin were staying. After lunch John and Caitlin set out for Fishguard in his powerful motorcar, with Janes and Dylan following rather more slowly in theirs. At the judging there was a lot of drink taken before both cars set out again, this time for Carmarthen. A breakdown forced Janes to stop, so the others went on together. John grew annoyed by Dylan's and Caitlin's obvious interest in each other. When Dylan demanded to be taken back to Laugharne, a fight broke out between the two men, leaving Dylan the loser, on his back in a pub carpark.

Caitlin had reached a point in her life where she was looking for something new, waiting for something to happen. She had long wanted to be a dancer. As a young girl she made her way to London to work in the chorus at the Palladium, but she was undisciplined and untrained. Courageous, exhibitionist, with artistic yearnings, she had little

The harbour at Fishguard, home to the National Eisteddfod in 1936 where Dylan continued his wooing of Caitlin

discernible talent. She gave performances in private houses, and she spent some time working in Paris, but it was obvious she was unlikely to be a success. Then she met Dylan. He was already well known as a poet, a rising star. Might she be able to satisfy her ambitions by uniting them with his?

Caitlin was very striking looking, ripe and sensuous, but with an aura of youth and innocence. Dylan was soon very much in love with her: she has 'seas of golden hair, two blue eyes, two brown arms, two

Caitlin, dancer and performer, photographed on the banks of the
Avon by Nora Summers, a friend and sometime lover of her mother

Dylan in the Gower garden of his friend Vernon Watkins in 1937 shortly after his marriage to Caitlin

dancing legs, is untidy and vague and un-reclamatory'. Seduced by a romantic notion of the artist and poet, and without any strong sense of direction for herself at this point, she seemed happy to take on the multiple role of his mistress, mother and muse. As long as he continued to write great poetry, she would willingly put up with the difficulties and insecurities of their life together. But when he spent more and more time on other work, or seemed not to be working at all, she began to feel she had been cheated, robbed of her own career and identity. Such feelings are understandable if disingenuous, an almost inevitable response to her position as his wife and mother of his three children, when he held all the cards and could be said to be dealing them irrationally and unfairly.

Dylan's expectations were equally precarious. From the start, he placed great importance on their remaining 'young and unwise'.

Oh I know we're not saints or virgins or lunatics; we know all the lust and lavatory jokes, and most of the dirty people; we can catch buses and count our change and cross the roads and talk real sentences. But our innocence goes awfully deep and our discreditable secret is that we don't know anything at all, and our horrid inner secret is that we don't care that we don't.

He liked to emphasize and capitalize on his weaknesses – he was small and lightly built, he was often ill, he never had any money. Now Caitlin was to be woven into this regressive fantasy. She must be innocent too, untouched by the world. It was true that she looked very young; he would discover only later that she was ten months older than he was. She was genuinely untroubled by social conventions and restraints; she would often sit silent, detached from what was going on around her. Yet Dylan was aware enough of her past life to know that she could not be as innocent as she looked. He certainly was not. By pretending otherwise, was he signalling to her his inability or, at least, his reluctance to take responsibility for himself and his life? For the present she went along with his fantasy, for she wanted him to be dependent on her. He did not yet recognize how much he needed her to be dependable.

Their courtship was roundabout and slow, hampered by lack of money, by their being very often apart: he was in Swansea and she was at her mother's house in Hampshire or with her father in County Galway. A change in Dylan's parents' circumstances may have helped bring matters to a head. At the end of 1936 D.J. Thomas had retired from teaching at Swansea Grammar School. The following spring he and his wife sold 5 Cwmdonkin Drive and moved to a smaller house in Bishopston on the outskirts of Swansea. Dylan lost his childhood home and his bolt hole in Wales. He would have to find a place of his own. What better solution than to set up house with Caitlin? He wrote to his parents from Cornwall where he and Caitlin were staying to tell them the 'Dylan-life-altering news', that he was on the point of getting married. He admitted to having no money, except for £3 saved to pay for the marriage licence. After the wedding Caitlin would have to return to Hampshire, and he would live in Wales 'until I can make just exactly enough money to keep us going until I make just exactly enough money again'. He knew that they were unlikely to approve. 'It may, & possibly does, sound a rash and mad scheme, but it satisfies us and it is all we ask for. I do hope it won't hurt you.' D.J. Thomas enlisted the help of his son-in-law, Nancy's husband, to try to prevent what he thought was a lunatic course of action, but efforts to persuade the Cornish registrar that he should not go ahead with the ceremony came to nothing. Doubtless remembering his own thwarted ambitions and fearing for his son's future, Dylan's father sent him £5. Caitlin is 'sufficiently like myself to care little or nothing for proprietary interests and absolutely nothing for the responsibilities of husbandly provision', Dylan assured his sister and her husband, but he asked them for 'a couple of quid' none the less. When Pamela Hansford Johnson wrote to congratulate him and asked what they would like as a wedding present, he suggested that she send them a pound. He could make light of their poverty

Dylan's parents' home in Bishopston. They moved here from Cwmdonkin Park when D.J. Thomas retired in late 1936.

and lack of prospects but, in time, what could be laughed off as a youthful affectation became a real and pressing problem. By early 1938, less than eight months after their 'pleasant and eccentric marriage' in Penzance, they were seriously short of funds.

From Cornwall they went straight to Swansea, staying first in a pub in the Mumbles and then, less happily, with Dylan's parents in Bishopston. The house was small, and Mrs Thomas and her daughter-in-law held rather different views of a wife's

Dylan and Caitlin, just married, 1937

role. For about six months they lived with Caitlin's mother in Hampshire. Dylan began writing more easily again, both poems and the first of the stories which he would publish as *Portrait of the Artist as a Young Dog*. But Mrs Macnamara could not be expected to support them indefinitely, and Dylan was beginning to miss his life and friends in Wales. He wrote to Richard Hughes to ask him if he knew of a cottage in Carmarthenshire which they could rent. Help was at hand: in early May 1938 the young couple moved into 'Eros', a small fisherman's cottage in Gosport Street, Laugharne.

Laugharne is the place now most closely associated with Dylan Thomas, thought of, in preference to Swansea, as his true home. In fact he settled in this 'timeless, mild, beguiling island of a town' more by chance than by design. Richard Hughes had found him a house he could afford, and he would also offer companionship, the use of a large library and, perhaps less willingly, the pleasures of a good wine cellar. Laugharne

Laugharne Castle, 'the colossal broken castle, owls asleep in the centuries, the same rooks talking as in Arthur's time'

was only fifteen miles from Carmarthen by winding road and about the same distance again from Swansea. Across the River Taf, connected by a tiny ferry, lay Llanstephan, Llanybri and Llangain, homelands of both Dylan's mother's and father's families. Yet the town remained isolated, set apart, an English-speaking enclave surrounded by countryside where Welsh was the first and everyday language. The people of Laugharne had a reputation for eccentricity and rowdiness of which they were proud.

...when you say in a nearby village or town that you come from this unique, this waylaying, old, lost Laugharne, where some people start to retire before they start to work and where longish journeys, of a few hundred yards, are often undertaken only on bicycles, then, oh! the wary edging away, the whispers and the whimpers, and nudges, the swift removal of portable objects!

'Let's get away while the going is good,' you hear.

'Laugharne's where they quarrel with boathooks.'

'All the women there's got web feet.'

'Mind out for the Evil Eye!'

'Never go there at the full moon!'

The bar of Brown's Hotel, Laugharne

Brown's Hotel in Laugharne's main street. Dylan spent a part of each day with the landlady, Ivy Williams. They both enjoyed gossip and scandal.

Laugharne fell into two distinct halves: the upper town was defined by the long main street, lined with shops and houses, at one end the church, at the other the ruined castle. It could claim a certain decayed grandeur. The lower town was more modest and lay at the bottom of a small hill, close by the shore. Here lived the families of the fishermen whose wives and children collected cockles on the sands at low tide. From Norman times Laugharne had had its own particular system of government, run by a body of strangely named officials presided over by the port reeve or mayor. In 1938 Richard Hughes was probably the town's best-known inhabitant. He lived in the upper town in the Castle

House, an attractive Georgian building which he had refurbished with the help of the architect Clough Williams-Ellis, and which overlooked the ruined castle on one side and the open mouth and headlands of the estuary behind. But without doubt the most powerful people in Laugharne were the Williams family. They owned a lot of property and they ran the principal pub, Brown's Hotel, the generators which supplied the town's electricity, and the bus and taxi services.

'Eros' was a small house, 'pokey and ugly, four rooms like stained boxes in a workman's and fisherman's row, with a garden leading down to mud and sea.' Damp marked the florid wallpaper, much of the furniture was

'Eros', Gosport Street, Laugharne, Dylan's
and Caitlin's first home

on its last legs, and the toilet was an earth closet. But Dylan and Caitlin seemed content. They had very little money, but they could live on credit, at least for short periods of time, and occasionally they were given presents of fish and vegetables. While Dylan was working, Caitlin went cockling on the sands near the house, or she would bathe in the estuary, go for long walks over Sir John's Hill or along the seashore. Both she and Dylan were of great interest to their neighbours. She refused to alter her habits to suit the strict manners and customs of Laugharne. She had no qualms about being seen in her purple housecoat, and Dylan would go to collect water from the outside tap wearing his pyjamas under an overcoat. At night the local boys would peer through the uncurtained windows of 'Eros' and report on what was going on inside. Caitlin found such close scrutiny restricting, but Dylan felt quite at home.

After three months they moved to 'Sea View', 'a tall and dignified house at the posh end of this small town', which they rented from the Williams family. 'Sea View' was lighter and more spacious, but it was unfurnished, so they set about acquiring furniture from relatives and friends. There was no electricity, and at night the house was lit by candles. Caitlin's famous stews, made from whatever combination of meat, fish or

vegetables was available to her, simmered all day on the range. They were still very hard up and she was pregnant – 'a very nice mistake, and neither of us worries at all'. One day followed another with little change of routine. In the morning Dylan worked a little, then he would have one or two drinks in the pub before lunch. In the afternoon he and Caitlin would often go to bed, sometimes just to keep warm, and he would read to her. After more work he would go back to the pub for the evening, to the Cross House Inn or to Brown's Hotel.

Caitlin would claim after Dylan's death that they had never once spent an evening at home in all the years they were married. Before they had children, this presented few problems for her. She may often have been bored by the conversation and found few people in the pub to interest her, but at least she was with Dylan and not obliged to stay in the house. She seemed to be happy with their way of life, although apparently this was not so. Even before the birth of their first child, she had begun to feel dissatisfied and unfulfilled and in need of other men and other relationships.

Dylan's concerns were of a different kind. Once again in a small room in Wales, isolated, his every need met, he was writing again. He had begun to revise the notebook poems which would make up half of his next

'Our innocence goes awfully deep, and our discreditable secret is that we don't know anything at all and... we don't care that we don't.'

collection, *The Map of Love*. But he was finding it difficult to write new poetry. The poem he wrote to mark his twenty-fourth birthday in October 1938 expresses his unease. His is a troubled voice, offering no prospect of easy resolution.

Twenty-four years remind the tears of my eyes.
(Bury the dead for fear that they walk to the
  grave in labour.)
In the groin of the natural doorway I
  crouched like a tailor
Sewing a shroud for a journey
By the light of the meat-eating sun.
Dressed to die, the sensual strut begun,
With my red veins full of money,
In the final direction of the elementary town
I advance for as long as forever is.

Money worries had helped stem the flow of poetry – 'I live from poem to mouth, and both suffer.' Prose was to prove a little easier, almost an indulgence, certainly an escape. He took up the suggestion made by his editor Richard Church, uncomfortable with the fantastic and surreal in his work, that he write something autobiographical. Richard Hughes had offered him the use of a gazebo in the grounds of the ruined castle beside his house. Perched above the sands and the rising and falling tides of the estuary, Dylan returned to his childhood and early years. The stories he wrote – 'all about Swansea life, the pubs, clubs, billiard salons, promenades, adolescence in the suburban nights, friendships, tempers, and humiliations' – would become *Portrait of the Artist as a Young Dog*, snapshots of his growth from observant,

Dylan and Caitlin in Brown's Hotel, Laugharne. They had moved to Laugharne in May 1938.

impressionable young boy to cub reporter, come of age, his hat at an angle, a cigarette in his mouth, tankard of beer in his hand. The background to the stories is familiar – the suburban villas of Swansea, Cwmdonkin Park, the streets and pubs down town, the sands of Swansea Bay, the long curving shore at Rhossili and, most emblematic, his aunt Annie's farm at Fernhill. His aunt had died in 1933, too soon for Dylan to understand his

One of Dylan's worksheets. In his painstaking search for the right word, he would make long lists, often using a thesaurus.

loss and her importance to him, but now, six years later, he was far enough away from the experiences of his childhood to have them in perspective. He had tried out and seen enough of life to want to understand who he was once and who he might yet be.

Fernhill was already part of a lost world. Seven years later he would reinvent it in his poem 'Fern Hill', in a lyrical fusion of his young self with farmhouse, animals, trees, birds, sky. Before he began to write his Fernhill story 'The Peaches', he revised 'After the Funeral', the poem which he had written at the time of his aunt's death, replacing the adolescent, cynical, self-centred view of her death with a sense of celebration and a recognition of how much she and the farm had meant to him as a child. He now understood how she had belonged to this place, how significant were the details of her private, individual world. It was, he now knew, a vital part of his own inner landscape.

But I, Ann's bard on a raised hearth, call all
The seas to service that her wood-tongued virtue
Babble like a bellbuoy over the hymning heads,
Bow down the walls of the ferned and foxy woods
That her love sing and swing through a brown chapel,
Bless her bent spirit with four, crossing birds,
Her flesh was meek as milk, but this skyward statue
With the wild breast and blessed and giant skull
Is carved from her in a room with a wet window
In a fiercely mourning house in a crooked year.
I know her scrubbed and sour humble hands
Lie with religion in their cramp, her threadbare
Whisper in a damp word, her wits drilled hollow,
Her fist of a face died clenched on a round pain;
And sculptured Ann is seventy years of stone.
These cloud-sopped, marble hands, this monumental
Argument of the hewn voice, gesture and psalm
Storm me forever over her grave until
The stuffed lung of the fox twitch and cry Love
And the strutting fern lay seeds on the black sill.

Dylan's story 'The Peaches' was based on fact, on the visit to the farm, as a paying guest, of his friend Jack. His aunt's attempts to impress Jack's wealthy mother – her offer of tinned peaches at teatime – go embarrassingly wrong. The gulf between the two worlds, of the town and the farm, too great for Jack and his mother, was one which Dylan had learned to cross.

> The front of the house was the single side of a black shell, and the arched door was the listening ear. I pushed the door open and walked into the passage out of the wind. I might have been walking into the hollow night and the wind, passing through a tall vertical shell on an island sea-shore. Then a door at the end of the passage opened; I saw the plates on the shelves, the lighted lamp on the long, oil-clothed table, 'Prepare to Meet thy God' over the fire-place, the smiling china dogs, the brown-stained settle, the grandmother clock, and I ran into the kitchen and into Annie's arms.
>
> There was a welcome then. The clock struck twelve as she kissed me, and I stood among the shining and striking like a prince taking off his disguise. One minute I was small and cold, skulking dead-scared down a black passage in my stiff, best suit, with my hollow belly thumping and my heart like a time bomb, clutching my grammar school cap, unfamiliar to myself, a snub-nosed story-teller lost in his own adventures and longing to be home; the next I was a royal nephew in smart town clothes, embraced and welcomed, standing in the snug centre of my stories and listening to the clocks announcing me. She hurried me to the seat in the side of the cavernous fireplace and took off my shoes. The bright lamps and the ceremonial gongs blazed and rang for me.

It became more and more important for Dylan to fuse present and past, to establish a safe place in which to anchor himself. All around him things were shifting and changing. In January 1939 Caitlin gave birth to their first child, a boy they named Llewelyn. He was born in Poole, near Caitlin's mother's home. For the present Dylan was not unhappy to be away from Laugharne – the debts he and Caitlin had run up could no longer be ignored, and he had left owing £30 which he was quite unable to repay. All his attempts to raise the money from publishers, agents and editors had failed. By May they were back in 'Sea View' with their new baby, 'a fat, round, bald, loud child with a spread nose and blue saucer eyes'. Caitlin was well, none the worse for her pregnancy, but Dylan had added 28 pounds in weight. He was only

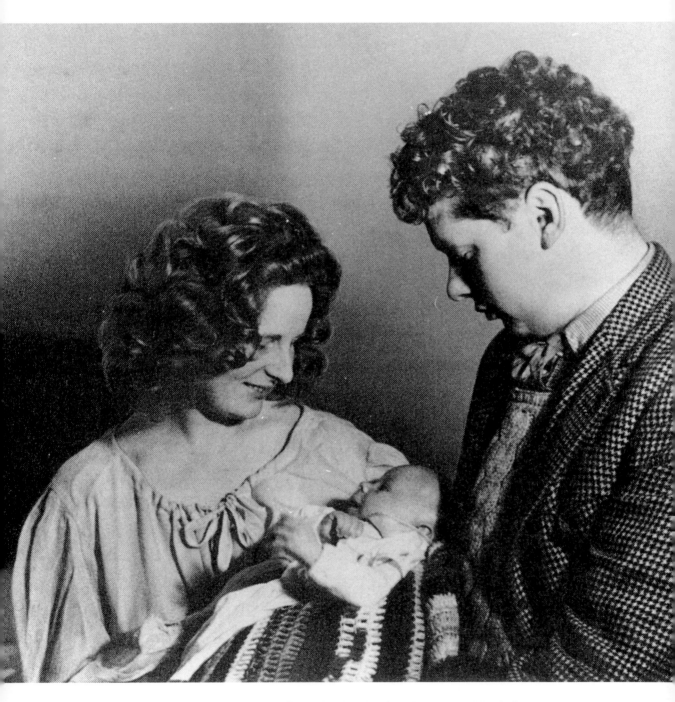

ABOVE *Caitlin and Dylan with their first child, Llewelyn, born in January 1939, 'a fat,
round, bald child with a spread nose and blue saucer eyes'*
PREVIOUS PAGE *The summer house, built into the wall of Laugharne Castle above the River
Taf, where Dylan wrote several of the stories for* Portrait of the Artist as a Young Dog

'Sea View', Laugharne, home for Dylan and Caitlin between 1938 and 1940, 'a tall and dignified house at the posh end of this small town'

25 years old, but already he had begun to look like the middle-aged man he would never become. He felt out of touch and out of place, no longer sure where he belonged. He reflected ruefully in a letter to Bert Trick that 'never again will I fit into Swansea quite so happily and comfortably as I did – for I'll be a hundred jokes and personal progressions behind all my friends'. He was a married man with a wife and child to support, but unable to earn enough to support them. The threat of war made it very unlikely that his prospects would improve. He had absolutely no intention of fighting or putting himself at risk. '...The Germans are not my enemies, I do not want to die or kill, freedom's only a word and I'm a thinking body.' He managed to avoid conscription on health grounds, but this meant that he would have to find some other kind of regular work.

The BBC had begun to pay him for radio scripts, but these might no longer be wanted. Paper would be rationed and book sales damaged. This was clear even before war was declared. His collection of stories and poems, *The Map of Love*, published in August 1939, was well enough received but it sold badly. *Portrait of the Artist as A Young Dog*, published the following April, was completely overwhelmed.

Dylan with John Davenport, good friend, fellow writer and drinking companion, photographed in 1952

BELOW *'Now their love lies a loss/And Love and his patients roar on a chain'*
OVERLEAF *Laugharne, 'this timeless, mild, beguiling island of a town'*

One thing was certain – he could not continue to live in Laugharne. In May 1940, with Caitlin and their little son, he left 'Sea View' for the last time, to stay first with his parents in Bishopston and then with Caitlin's mother in Hampshire. He took up John Davenport's invitation and joined a number of writers and musicians at his house near Chippenham in Gloucestershire. Davenport and he worked together on 'a fantastic thriller'. Their fellow-guests were interesting and entertaining. With Caitlin he explored the countryside on bicycles while bombs rained on London and Swansea. But this was to be a very brief respite. Caitlin's entanglement with another of the guests, William Glock, deeply shocked Dylan and forced him to recognize that she was not the devoted, faithful wife he wanted and needed. His marriage was not the stable rock on which he could confidently build his life and work. 'Very muddled and unhappy', homeless, in debt, his work and purpose as a poet undermined by the war, he fled back to Wales.

CHAPTER 4

Deaths and Entrances

'We are now quite homeless. What I need is just enough to let me look around for a cottage somewhere in Wales where we can begin again to try to live and work alone. We could, perhaps, get along for a little time in London – I don't know how – but obviously we couldn't have our baby there...There's sure to be a cottage in Pembrokeshire or Carmarthenshire I could hire cheaply, but as it is I can't even go to look for it let alone pay the first month or so's rent.'

FOR DYLAN AND Caitlin, at the end of 1940, the outlook was bleak. Having left Laugharne to escape their debts, they were forced to lodge with Dylan's parents in Bishopston, 'God's least favourite place', where they were cooped up in a small house with baby Llewelyn, now almost two years old, and with no money which would have allowed at least an occasional escape into Swansea, to the cinema or pub. The days were dull and short, the weather cold. One week into the new year a water pipe in the cottage burst, flooding the parlour. Caitlin, in a man's hat, ran to and fro with a mop while Dylan sat looking on, trying to write. Such disorder was not unusual: they were soon to be constantly on the move between Wales and London in search of work and a place to live, dodging German bombs, always hard up, appealing to any and all likely parties for money.

Dylan was still determined that he would not become caught up in the war. He had been declared unfit for military service, but

Dylan painted at 'Sea View', Laugharne, in 1940 by Rupert Shephard

he was afraid that he could be made to do uncongenial war work. The life of a munitions worker held no attractions for him – 'deary me I'd rather be a poet any day and live on guile and beer'. One way of earning some money suggested itself. Asked by the antiquarian book dealer Bertram Rota if he had any manuscripts he would be willing to sell, he decided to part with the four notebooks into which he had copied the poems he was writing in Swansea between 1930 and 1934. There is no way of knowing how seriously he took this decision, if he saw it simply as a way of getting some money, or if he was consciously closing a period of his life, severing his ties with 'the Rimbaud of Cwmdonkin Drive'. He had told his mother years before that he would one day be as good a poet as Keats. He was now twenty-six years old, close to the age Keats was when he died. Poems came less easily to him than before; he knew that he was losing touch with his young self. He may have seen the sale as a fresh start.

In other ways the present was blotting out his past. In February 1941 Swansea was heavily bombed and much of the town centre destroyed. Dylan and Caitlin travelled in from Bishopston to look at the damage done. Standing in the rubble of the devastated streets, he felt that a large part of his childhood had been wiped out. The raids worried his parents, and they began to think of leaving Bishopston, now too close to Swansea for comfort. Dylan and Caitlin were very happy to accept an invitation from Frances Hughes to stay with her in the Castle House in Laugharne while her husband, who was working for the Admiralty, was away from home. When he came back to Laugharne on leave, Richard Hughes was not too pleased to find the Thomases there. As ever, they had no money. Dylan was trying to remedy this by selling first editions of novels through Bertram Rota. Hughes may well have suspected that these came from his own library. Dylan never had any qualms about requisitioning the property of his friends; he borrowed their clothes without their consent and returned them as rarely as he did the money they lent him. For the present, Vernon Watkins was his main banker. He had enlisted and was working for RAF Intelligence. His patience must surely have been tried on occasions by his improvident friend. At the end of a letter thanking him for the half-crown he had just sent, Dylan blithely asks for more.

Here we are, safe and quiet, and should be happy as cabbages, but it's hard – for me – without a single hour's, half-hour's, minute's, going out in the long, social evening...I get in such a nagged, impotent, messy state when I'm like this; sit and snap and worry all day; can't be easy, can't work hard, just sit by myself saying 'Fuck it' in a flat voice. I do like that wonderful independence of being able to walk across the road any time and buy an envelope or some Vim.

He went with Caitlin to London in mid-August; he had to find a job. He failed to interest a publisher in the novel, *Adventures in the Skin Trade*, which he had been working on since the spring, but he began to look for an opening in the film business as a script writer and was told that there might be work for him in the near future. In the meantime he and Caitlin had to live on promises. They felt like 'prisoners in a live melodrama', in 'stinking, friendless London' without the money to go out to restaurants or pubs and, presumably, unable to find anyone who would pay for them. Happily, by the end of the year, he was on the payroll of Donald Taylor's Strand Film Company, which was making documentary films for the Ministry of Information. Work for Strand counted as a 'reserved occupation', so putting an end to Dylan's fears that he might be called up, and Donald Taylor was a very understanding boss. As long as scripts were delivered on schedule, they could be written anywhere,

in the office in London or, in Dylan's case, in Wales. He had had a passion for films from his early days in Swansea, when he and his friends would go to the Uplands cinema where they 'whooped for the scalping Indians...and banged for the rustlers' guns'. At Strand he very quickly gained a good knowledge and understanding of film technique. Sometimes he would be bored by the work, and he and his colleague Julian Maclaren-Ross would kill time discussing the feature films they really wanted to write instead of the propaganda documentaries they were working on – *New Towns For Old*, *Battle for Freedom*, *A Soldier Comes Home* and others. But he never denigrated his work for Strand. Indeed it was a godsend. At first he was paid £8 per week; this rose to £10 and, later, to £20 plus expenses, money which was vital to him during these years.

But Caitlin disliked and resented what Dylan liked to call 'my war work'. She thought it was corrupting him, taking him away from poetry and his own writing. She also suspected that a lot of the time he was in London he was not really working but talking and drinking with his colleagues, and possibly spending time with women. She may have recognized his dilemma, but she would not accept it. He had to earn a living, but he could not do this through poetry alone. While he was working at Strand, she

spent a lot of her time in Laugharne or further west in Cardiganshire, in Talsarn, a remote village in the valley of the River Aeron. (They would name their daughter, Aeronwy, after this river. A little to the south lay the River Marlais, one of the sources of Dylan's second name.) Caitlin stayed with Vera, a childhood friend of Dylan in Swansea. Her husband was away fighting and she was glad of company. Dylan visited them when he could. The journey from London to the west of Wales in wartime was tedious and slow but, once there, he could write and live at a more reasonable pace. Food rationing in country districts was less stringent. 'I have been here for over a week with Caitlin, with milk and mild and cheese and eggs, and I feel fit as a fiddle only bigger.'

Even after they had moved into a studio flat in Manresa Road in Chelsea, Dylan and Caitlin often lived apart. They had managed to find only one room with a glass roof, which was not ideal in wartime, and even less so when Aeronwy was born in March 1943. Nor was it suitable for Dylan, for there was nowhere he could be alone and quiet. Caitlis had little choice but to take Aeronwy off to Laugharne, from where she could visit Dylan's parents, or go to Vera in Talsarn. In her absence Dylan wrote her pleading, impassioned letters.

ABOVE *Dylan and Caitlin with Aeronwy, born in March 1943*

LEFT *Bridge over the River Aeron, Cardiganshire. Dylan and Caitlin called their daughter Aeronwy after the river.*

It has never been so useless and lonely away from you as it is this time; there is nothing to live for without you, except for your return or when I can [come] down to Laugharne which must, somehow, be this week because I love you far more than ever and I will not exist without your love and loveliness, darling, so please write and tell me you miss me, too, and love me, and think of us being, soon, together for ever again. By the time you get this, you'll also have got, I hope, *a bit more money* which I will wire either tonight or tomorrow morning.

Dylan prepares for a radio broadcast. He proved to be a very natural but professional performer.

He ended the same letter to her, 'Every bit of my love to you, every substance & shadow of it, every look & thought & word.' He knew very well that this was only partly true. Caitlin was necessary to him; he could not imagine life without her, but he was no longer faithful to her, and he knew that she was not faithful to him. He wrote telling her what she may have wanted to hear, but which she no longer believed. He wrote as if his torrent of words would bind her to him, would mask and mend the faults in their relationship.

Another source of work and income offered itself when, early in 1943, Dylan recorded his first radio broadcast for the BBC, 'Reminiscences of Childhood'. At first he wanted to call this 'Nostalgia for an Ugly Town'. He talked about his childhood in suburban Swansea – in Cwmdonkin Park, at nursery school, in the lane between home and school, where the children would tell tales and where his fanciful boast that he could fly took wing and bore him aloft over school, trees, chimneys, dockyards and town. But, he ended,

This is only a dream. The ugly, lovely, at least to me, town is alive, exciting and real though war has made a hideous hole in it. I do not need to remember a dream. The reality is there. The fine live people, the spirit of Wales itself.

It seems this last sentence was not in his original script. It was added to conform with the unwritten rule that all talks on the BBC Welsh Service should end with a reference to the spirit of Wales. Nostalgia came easily to Dylan; the tone of his talk – of bemused, affectionate reminiscence – was one he would use often and to great effect. But doffing his cap to the people of Wales would not have been part of his plan; this kind of sentimental nationalism was not for him. His relationship with his country was much deeper and more complex.

Caitlin grew more and more disenchanted; Dylan fell ill. A life divided between wartime London and rural Wales suited neither of them. Driven out of town by more frequent bombing in early 1944, they moved to the English south coast, to a cottage in Bosham on the edge of Chichester Harbour. From here they went to stay with Donald Taylor near Slough, to the west of London. July 1944 saw them once again in Wales, staying with Dylan's parents who had moved to Blaen Cwm near Llangain, across the estuary from Laugharne, to one of a pair of cottages which Florence Thomas had inherited from her sister Dosie. Next door were an unmarried brother and sister. All of them felt they would be safer away from Swansea and any more bombing. But living in the country, so near his wife's relatives and starved of intelligent conversation, did not improve D.J. Thomas's temper or disposition.

Dylan's visits may have brought some relief, although the house was small and it must have been hard to accommodate two more adults and two young children. '...we'll stay here, getting on my father – for he's one bald nerve – until we find a house, a flat, a room, a sty, a release.' Dylan and Caitlin felt little affection for Llangain:

...everyone goes into the pubs sideways, & the dogs piss only on back doors, and there are more unwanted babies shoved up the chimneys than there are used french letters in the offertory boxes. It's a mean place but near Laugharne.

And it was a place in which he could begin writing again. It had been a long time since he had written any poetry; now he completed 'Vision and Prayer', which had remained unfinished all through the war years, and another of his birthday poems, 'Poem in October'. It looked as if living in

Fishguard Bay. Dylan came to the National Eisteddfod in Fishguard, with Caitlin and Augustus John, in 1936.

New Quay on the edge of Cardigan Bay, the 'cliff-perched town' with 'salt-white houses dangling over water', was a source for Llareggub in Under Milk Wood.

Wales might again refresh and inspire him, and this was indeed to be the case. Dylan and Caitlin moved to New Quay in the late summer of the same year; the nine months spent there were among his most productive.

They rented a timber and asbestos bungalow called 'Majoda' on the cliffs overlooking Cardigan Bay and the sea:

Solva Harbour, one of the places in Wales which Dylan thought of nostalgically when he was in London.

'It's in a really wonderful bit of the bay, with a beach of its own. Terrific...The name is made of the beginnings of the names of the three children of the man who built the questionable house. I may alter the name to Cattlewdylaer.'

'Majoda' was outside the town, about a mile along the coast road. The rent was only one pound per week, but there was no electricity and no mains water. The nearest building was another bungalow which was occupied by Vera, their friend from Talsarn, and her baby daughter. New Quay, on the side of the bay, its steep main street running down to a harbour, was a more sophisticated town than Laugharne; a large proportion of its residents were retired and middle class. It soon became known that there was a poet living in the house on the cliff, but Dylan and Caitlin provoked little other comment. Their life soon took on the familiar routine. Dylan would write mostly in the afternoon, and evenings would be spent in a local pub, usually the Black Lion, with one-year-old Aeronwy tucked up in the landlady's bed upstairs. It was not easy to work in the bungalow – the rooms were small and the walls paper-thin, so he rented a room nearby. He was working on film scripts for Donald Taylor; he wrote several poems, and a radio script, 'Quite Early One Morning', which he recorded in December 1944. He seemed to be at ease, out of danger, in this small, quiet Welsh town.

> There is no news here: a woman called Mrs. Prosser died in agony last week, there has been a coroner's inquest on a drowned coastguard (verdict suicide), Vera's cat was wounded by a rabbit & died, all night long we hear rabbits shrieking like babies in the steel jaws in the hedges, Caitlin killed five mice in one day by traps, but, still, I am quite happy and looking forward to a gross, obscene and extremely painful middle-age.

He went back and forward to London, but not very often, for it was a long journey and he had no wish to get caught up in the Blitz. Usually he went alone, coming back to Caitlin 'to be nursed and cursed'. She was unhappy about the time he spent away, accusing him of irresponsibility, suspecting that he spent far more money on himself and his friends in London than he brought back for his family. Dylan made light of her accusations:

> Back in the bosom, repentant and blood-
>   shot,
> Under the draper-sly skies,
> I try to forget my week in the mudpot
> And cottonwool it in lies;

He found that he could not so lightly pass off

his behaviour to Vernon Watkins and his wife, Gwen. Dylan had agreed to be best man at their wedding, but he failed to show up. Weeks afterwards he wrote to apologize and to explain why – he had set out for the church only to find that he could not remember its name. Months later he offered a more plausible explanation:

> I have found, increasingly as time goes on, or around, or backwards, or stays quite still as the brain races, the heart absorbs and expels, and the arteries harden, that the problems of physical life, of social contact, of daily posture and armour, of the choice between dissipations, of the abhorred needs enforced by a reluctance to 'miss anything', that old fear of death, are as insoluble to me as those of the spirit. In few and fewer poems I can despair and, at rare moments, exult with the big last, but the first force me every moment to make quick decisions and thus to plunge me into little hells and rubbishes at which I rebel with a kind of truculent acceptance. The ordinary moments of walking up village streets, opening doors or letters, speaking good-days to friends or strangers, looking out of windows, making telephone calls, are so inexplicably (to me) dangerous that I am trembling all over before I get out of bed in the mornings to meet them.

He claimed to feel this disequilibrium most acutely in London, 'broken on a wheel of streets and faces' but, he admitted, he might well be 'just as broken in the peace – what peace? – of the country, hysterical in my composure, hyena-ish in my vegetabledom'. Vernon Watkins seems to have accepted his apology, and it may be that Dylan was being completely straight and honest. His powers of self-analysis were considerable. Unfortunately they rarely brought him to any point of resolution or action. He had often taken cover behind stories of illness and bad luck. The doggerel verses and the letter of confession served the same end – both enabled him to avoid responsibility for his actions.

Of the 25 poems in *Deaths and Entrances*, published in February 1946, about a third were written or revised in New Quay, including 'A Refusal to Mourn the Death, by Fire, of a Child in London', 'Vision and Prayer' and 'Fern Hill'. His new radio script, 'Quite Early One Morning', was an imaginative portrait of the town. Dylan had an excellent eye for small details and incidents, an ability to infuse the ordinary with drama, which made him at times an unreliable witness but always a most engaging raconteur. In his radio broadcasts he married his powers of observation and expression with his considerable talent as a reader and actor. Like 'an

inquisitive shadow', he walked through the streets of New Quay in the early morning before anyone was awake, piling up images for his listeners and painting a picture of the town – the zinc-roofed chapel, the quay empty but for gulls and capstans 'like small men in tubular trousers', the police station with its roof 'black as a helmet'; salt-white houses dangling over the water, bow-windowed villas, unsteady hill streets and, behind the windows of the front parlours, the 'tasselled table-cloths, stuffed pheasants, ferns in pots, fading photographs of the bearded and censorious dead, autograph albums with a lock of limp and colourless beribboned hair lolling out between the thick black boards'.

Later, when he was writing *Under Milk Wood*, New Quay was very much in Dylan's mind. (The seaside town is physically much closer to Llareggub than is Laugharne.) But he was not to spend enough time there to get to know the people really well. A dramatic incident in March 1945 brought his stay there to a close. This began with a disagreement in the Black Lion where he was drinking with some of his film colleagues. Somehow they got into an argument with their neighbour Vera's husband, an army captain who had come home after a very dangerous tour of duty in Greece to find his wife living in great intimacy with Dylan and

Dylan and his mother in 1952 at Fernhill, which he visited often as a child, 'green and carefree, famous among the barns/About the happy yard and singing as the farm was home'.

Caitlin. She was short of money which, he suspected, was due to this friendship. Dylan and his friends left the pub and went back to 'Majoda'; the captain went to his house next door and equipped himself with an automatic and a hand grenade. Dylan's accounts of what happened next varied from telling to telling, but it seems certain that several

shots were fired both at and inside the bungalow, fortunately missing everyone. Next the captain threatened them with the hand grenade, but he did not pull the pin and, finally, he went away. The police were called and Dylan and Caitlin had to give evidence at a trial where the judge decided that there was not enough evidence to bring a charge.

Dylan was sorry to leave New Quay. It had been a haven, a place apart. At once worries began to gather about him thick and fast. Money was a problem, but more distressing was his father's poor health; he had serious heart problems and was in pain. Dylan and his family were once again without a home of their own, at Blaen Cwm in 'a house too full of Thomases' – father, mother, uncles, aunts, cousins, children – with no privacy, too much noise. He could escape to London for his film work, but then had to travel for up to eight hours to spend the weekend with his family. He quickly lost all sense of harmony with his Welsh surroundings; he was no longer sure he wanted to continue living in Wales. He began to talk about moving to America, of leaving the country completely. In flight from the present he turned once again to the past, and in December 1945 he wrote and recorded 'Memories of Christmas', a heavily nostalgic account of childhood Christmases in Swansea. (Later from this he would fashion one of his best-loved works, 'A Child's Christmas in Wales'.) He explored the same past time in a new poem, 'Fern Hill'. Blaen Cwm was only a few miles away from his aunt's farm. It was consoling to look back to a time and place when he felt at one with his surroundings, to days of pure sensation and innocence when he gave no thought to what lay ahead.

Nothing I cared, in the lamb white days, that time would take me
Up to the swallow thronged loft by the shadow of my hand,
 In the moon that is always rising,
  Nor that riding to sleep
 I should hear him fly with the high fields
And wake to the farm forever fled from the childless land.
Oh as I was young and easy in the mercy of his means,
  Time held me green and dying
 Though I sang in my chains like the sea.

This year, 1945, was the last really productive year of Dylan's life. His next book, *Deaths and Entrances*, was already in proof. With the end of the war, the Strand film company was wound up, but he moved on to work for another company, Gainsborough. He was very involved with the BBC, script writing, reading his own and other writers' work, and playing small acting parts. By the end of the year he and Caitlin had left Wales once more; they were not to live there again for four years. They spent the winter in London, with no settled address or reliable income, until early in 1946 when they made their way to Holywell Ford, the Oxford home of A.J.P. Taylor and his wife Margaret. Their house belonged to Magdalen College where he was a history lecturer. In the garden, on the banks of the Cherwell, there was a summer-house which became the Thomases' home. Alan Taylor quickly grew disenchanted with the poet at the bottom of his garden, but Margaret devoted a great deal of her time and money to him. In fact she was to be his landlord and provider for the rest of Dylan's life, a very generous, if sometimes too intrusive patron whom he and Caitlin grew to resent and to mock, but someone they could not do without. A summer-house on a river bank, with spring in the air, was preferable to a basement flat in the city. There would be time to listen and to think,

and the possibility of writing something important once again. But soon Dylan began to find excuses for inactivity: '...it is hard here with peace and no room, spring outside the window and the gascooker behind the back, sleep, food, loud wireless, broom and brush all in one kiosk, stunted bathing-hut or square milkbottle.'

Margaret came to his rescue, providing him with a wooden caravan in which to write. During 1946 he was working principally for the BBC. He travelled very often between Oxford and London, a much easier journey than the one from Wales, but these trips were no more lucrative. This was the period of his greatest fame in the pubs and bars of Soho. He was by now such a well-known figure that people would go to particular pubs to seek him out. At the end of an evening spent drinking and talking, he was often too tired or too late to get the last train home. He would take a taxi, or he would curl up in bed with anyone who would have him. Neither solution pleased Caitlin.

Dylan chose to regard the summer-house as a temporary home until another could be found for him in America, but for the moment nothing presented itself. Several of his friends, Edith Sitwell for one, were appalled at the thought of the penniless Thomases setting out across the Atlantic. They knew that Dylan was very unlikely to

Dylan with Caitlin – poet, script writer and broadcaster, public man

be able to earn a living and, at the same time, continue writing in America when he was failing to do just that in England. He had taken refuge in an impractical dream. He knew that he had little power of choice: 'I don't know what my plans are yet; they depend on money, and not on mine.' The winter of 1946 was a particularly cold one. England was still marked by the war; there were food and fuel shortages and power failures. The summer-house was not intended for such conditions. Here 'life is feverish', Dylan complained.

In February 1947 he went back to Swansea to research another broadcast, 'Return Journey', an exploration and evocation of the Swansea he knew as a boy and a young man.

Heavy bombing had irrevocably changed parts of the town, but it is not the physical changes, the loss of familiar streets and shops, which reverberate through his script, but the recognition that the young reporter who drank in the Three Lamps or sat talking with his friends in the Kardomah café, the schoolboy who slipped irreverent words into the morning hymns, the young lad who mooched around the dunes or called out to girls on the promenade, the child from dame school who played in Cwmdonkin Park, they had all gone for ever.

PARK-KEEPER: Oh yes, yes, I knew him well. He used to climb the reservoir railings and pelt the old swans. Run like a billygoat over the grass you should keep off. Cut branches off the trees. Carve words on the benches. Pull up moss in the rockery, go snip, snip through the dahlias. Fight in the bandstand. Climb the elms and moon up the top like an owl. Light fires in the bushes. Play on the green bank. Oh yes, I knew him well. I think he was happy all the time. I've known him by the thousands.

NARRATOR: We had reached the last gate. Dusk drew around us and the town. I said: What has become of him now?

PARK-KEEPER: Dead.

NARRATOR: The Park-keeper said:

[THE PARK BELL RINGS]

PARK-KEEPER: Dead...Dead...Dead...Dead...Dead...Dead.

Thanks to the efforts of Edith Sitwell and a generous travel grant given him by the Society of Authors, Dylan, Caitlin, her sister Brigit and their children were able to set out for Italy in the spring of 1947. Probably the last thing Dylan needed was a trip abroad; he would have done better to settle, to stay in one place. But Italy was warm – later in the summer, much too warm for him – and offered food and wine and a way of life totally foreign to post-war England. They stayed first in a pension in Rapallo – 'we need,' he wrote to Margaret Taylor, 'a small house to fill, cook in, work in, where children can be noisy, where we can make a rhythm and a way of our own.' They moved on to a house overlooking Florence and, finally, to Elba. All this time Margaret Taylor was working on their behalf, looking out for a more suitable English home for them. Dylan had had to put aside his hope of escaping to America; now he wanted a house in or near Oxford, indeed anywhere as long as it was a house of his own. 'I am domestic as a slipper. I want somewhere of my own, I am old enough now, I want a house to shout, sleep and work in.' He was delighted when she wrote to tell him that she had bought a cottage, rather inappropriately called the Manor House, in the village of South Leigh between Witney and Oxford.

...the house, the home, the haven, the pound-a-week Manor! Thank you with all my heart, from the depth of my teapot, from the marrow of my slippers warm before the fire, for finding a house for us. It is what I most want. It sounds *good*. 20 minutes from Oxford, ten from Witney, a Free House in the village, a kind old couple, fields, a garden: all I want's a new body and an alchemist's primer.

By September Dylan and his family, with cat and dog, had settled into their new home. The caravan was brought from Oxford and parked in the garden so that he could have a quiet place to work. South Leigh was an unpretentious village: Dylan and Caitlin were accepted and fitted in well. He travelled to London for work; she would put him to bed with bread and milk when he returned exhausted. Life should have been good, but they often quarrelled – over money and his drinking and socializing in London. Arguments would lead to scuffles and then to blows and, usually, to dramatic reconciliations. His earnings at this time were good, enough to keep them out of trouble. He was being given a lot to do by the BBC – he was, for instance, one of the readers for the Third Programme's production of Milton's *Paradise Lost*. He was also writing and being paid for film scripts. But within weeks they were living on credit. After the 'momentary affluence' of their time in Italy, they were back once again to hand-to-mouth, day-by-day living. It was no easier for being familiar. South Leigh was a small place, and they were afraid of losing the confidence and trust of their new neighbours.

Their situation was made worse by the illness of both Dylan's parents. Not only was D.J. Thomas's health worsening: Florence Thomas had fallen and broken her knee and

BELOW *The Boat House, as it was when Dylan and Caitlin lived there. At high tide the river lapped the back of the house.*

RIGHT *The Boat House today, encircled by a strong wall*

she too had to be cared for. Dylan's sister Nancy, who had divorced and remarried, was living in Devon and she took some of the burden. Dylan spent a week in Laugharne over Easter, visiting his mother in a hospital nearby. He was glad to be back but, at first, expressed no wish to return there to live. But as time went on this changed: 'Engulfed, as

ever, in domestic mishaps and sicknesses', with Margaret Taylor a too-frequent visitor, and London with its distractions only a short journey away, he turned again for help to Wales.

He moved back for the last time in May 1949. Margaret Taylor had bought the Boat House in Laugharne for £2500 so that she

The living room of the Boat House, as it is today

could rent it to them. Dylan, at least, felt that this return to Wales, and to a place he knew and loved, offered a chance of happiness. They would be secure as never before in a house which, although not their own, was very close to being so. Caitlin was pregnant, expecting their third child: when they had lived in Laugharne before, he had done good work and they had been happy. The move was a complicated one, for Dylan's parents had first to be settled into the house he had rented for them in the main street, directly opposite Brown's Hotel. He could easily visit them there, and his mother would be able to see him going to and from the pub. He and his family would live only a few minutes' walk away, on the edge of the town a little way down a narrow lane, then called Cliff Walk. Their home, the Boat House, sat by itself on the side of the estuary, suspended between the low sandstone cliff and the waters of the River Taf below. The roof of the house was almost level with the path above; at high tide the river lapped at the foot of the walls and flowed into the little harbour at the back of the house. It was not in very good condition; it was damp, without running water, and too often visited by rats. It could only be reached by a steep path. There were six rooms and a kitchen on three floors, not an ideal home in any sense for a family with very young

The Pelican, Dylan's parents' home in Laugharne during his final years there

children, but Caitlin managed to make it welcoming with pictures from magazines pinned to the walls and fires on chilly days.

Dylan planned to spend a part of each day in his writing shed, a wooden hut which had once been a garage, a little way along Cliff Walk. Alone, above the waters and sands of the estuary, sheltered by bushes and trees, he could write, read, dream or doze undisturbed. In the shed there was a table, a chair, a few books and, on the walls, reproductions and photographs of Walt Whitman, Thomas Hardy, D.H. Lawrence, W.H. Auden, William Blake, a painting by Modigliani, some female nudes; on the floor, discarded worksheets and drafts of work in progress. Through the window, to the east, he could see the ferryman working on the stretch of water separating Laugharne from Llanstephan and Llanybri; he could look across to the fields and farms around Pentowin. To the south rose Sir John's Hill, behind the muddy, tussocky foreshore of the lower town. When the tide was out fishing boats lay beached on the sand; at high water they lurched and bobbed in the fast stream.

In the first weeks Dylan wrote a new poem, 'Over Sir John's Hill', capturing the sights and scenes from his window, not simply to celebrate them, but to weave into this pastoral world of hillside and seascape his themes of impermanence and death.

ABOVE *Cliff Walk – now known as Dylan's Walk – from Laugharne to the Boat House, along the shore of the estuary*
RIGHT *Laugharne, the Boat House and Sir John's Hill, from Llanybri church on the other side of the estuary*

Over Sir John's hill,

The hawk on fire hangs still;

In a hoisted cloud, at drop of dusk, he pulls to his claws

And gallows, up the rays of his eyes the small birds of the bay

And the shrill child's play

Wars

Of the sparrows and such who swansing, dusk, in wrangling hedges.

And blithely they squawk

To fiery tyburn over the wrestle of elms until

The flash the noosed hawk

Crashes, and slowly the fishing holy stalking heron

In the river Towy below bows his tilted headstone.

Dylan playing cards with Ivy and Ebi Williams,
owners of Brown's Hotel, Laugharne

He also commemorated his homecoming in his next broadcast, 'Living In Wales'. This displayed little of the fantastical exuberance of his previous radio scripts: he seemed to want to tell his listeners that he was much more certain that he did not want to be in England, living among strangers, breathing alien air, than that he wanted to be in Wales. The picture he painted of his native land was, to say the least, colourless: he remembered the hollow sounds of a Welsh Sunday, the rebuking chapel, the bleak, empty front parlours, the flat, sad estuary sands. Convinced that he cannot fully be himself unless he is living in the place where he belongs, he returns, only to find little difference, to discover that everything is essentially the same. 'I know that I am home again because I feel just as I felt when I was not at home, only more so.'

Yet life in Laugharne suited Dylan very well, much more than it did Caitlin. People did not approve of her. They found her behaviour indiscreet, were shocked by her brightly coloured clothes, disliked her drinking and dancing, and were appalled by the

noisy and public rows she had with her husband, and her free and easy way with other men. Dylan slipped comfortably back into his familiar routines. In the morning he visited his parents, to chat and to do the crossword with his father. Afterwards he would cross the street to talk to Ivy Williams in the kitchen of Brown's Hotel, have a beer and listen to all the latest gossip. Then it was time for lunch, which he would eat alone, never at the same time as his family. He spent the afternoon in his writing shed. When Caitlin and the children passed by on their walks they could hear him muttering, reading aloud what he was writing, trying out the sounds and rhythms of his words.

In July 1949, Caitlin gave birth to a son. He was given both an Irish name, Colm, and a Welsh one, Garan, meaning heron, a bird frequently seen in the estuary and one which seemed to have a special significance for Dylan. Caitlin did not recover so quickly from this pregnancy as she had in the past – Dylan felt she looked thin and pale. He too was unwell, suffering with painful gout and, at one point, what he called a breakdown. He also had frequent falls, which resulted in broken or bruised arms and ribs. He would blame these on the rough, unfinished pathways of Laugharne. His return to the Boat House after his evening's drinking was fraught with danger. His mother would keep watch until he had safely navigated his way down the steps of Brown's Hotel, but she lost sight of him when he turned off the main street towards Cliff Walk and the steep path down to the Boat House. From that point he was on his own, in the dark.

In spite of his expectations and good intentions, within a very short time Dylan's life was once more unravelling, spinning out of control. Work was planned and promised but not delivered, letters were written and not posted. Money was a continuing problem; a young baby put further pressure on his relationship with Caitlin; his father's condition grew worse. Soon he owed a quarter year's rent on his parents' house, his son Llewelyn's school fees for the past term, and money to shopkeepers and tradesmen in Laugharne, a community so intimate that it was impossible to keep such a thing secret. He found once again that living in a small town had its drawbacks: he soon felt restricted, hemmed in. From time to time he would voice his frustration, decrying the unstimulating conversation in the pubs, declaring that he was bored with talk of swedes and bulldozers, the date of Princess Margaret's birthday, the price of geese. But more often than not he was happy playing darts and chatting to the other customers, all of whom he got to know well. He chose to spend time with them, away from his work

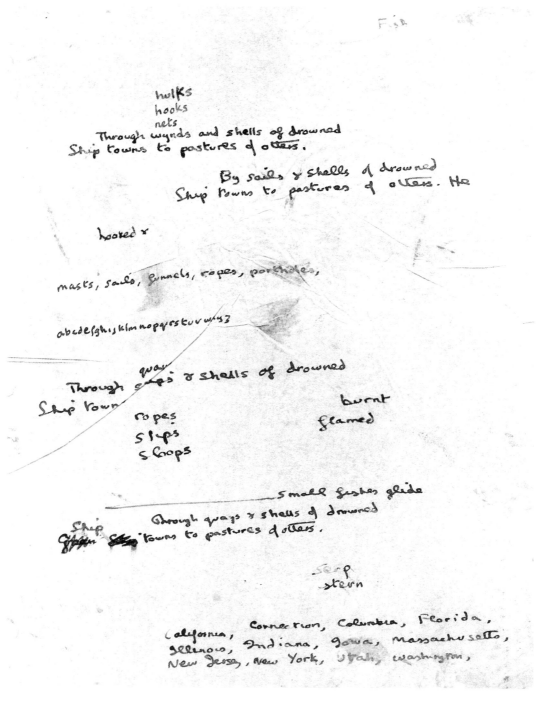

*One of Dylan's worksheets for 'Poem on his Birthday' which he
finished in 1951. While he worked on the poem, he made a list of
towns to visit on his second American tour the following year.*

and his family, to live what he called a 'seesaw life'. He complained that he was penniless, that his only wish was to write big poems, but on his table were only unfinished lines, odd words, nothing complete. He felt thwarted, prevented from doing what he really wanted to do, but he was incapable of finding a way out of his impasse. He took no steps, made no changes to his way of life which would have relieved the pressure of debt.

In October of 1949 he was to be the guest of honour at the annual dinner of the Swansea branch of the British Medical Association, but on the night he failed to appear. The letter of apology and explanation which he wrote afterwards was a literary *tour de force*. This was not an isolated incident, the only time he would write to explain some failure or rudeness, putting enough energy, ingenuity and imagination into the letter as would (one imagines) have fired and fuelled a poem. Was his ragged, disorganized life his best excuse? Was he embracing chaos so as to hide his inability to write, his failure to produce any significant new poetry? After another fall in November 1949, he wrote to Margaret Taylor that it was a convenient, if nasty way of avoiding finishing a piece of work. 'I may, after all, break my neck as a final procrastination.' Was the gulf now so great between his aims and achievements

that he could only fill it with illness, debts, arguments, talk and drink?

Shortly after he returned to Laugharne, Dylan received an invitation from John Brinnin, newly appointed director of the Poetry Center in New York, asking him to America. Brinnin would pay him to read his poems at the Center, and he would organize readings for him in other parts of the country. Dylan accepted his invitation with alacrity, suggesting that he come early in 1950 and stay for up to three months. On this, and three subsequent visits to America, he lived in an unreal world of drink, conversation, little sleep and constant movement. His readings were a great success, but many of the social events he attended before and after them were a disaster. He came to a country where the cult of celebrity was already well established, and he fell into its trap. 'Dylan Thomas', the public figure, usurped Dylan Thomas the man. He earned good money, but he was unable to keep it: it seemed to melt away in his hands. He gave Caitlin a heavily edited account of what he was doing, emphasizing how exhausting it all was – he said that on this first trip he had visited more than forty universities – not dwelling on the partying and the adulation, not mentioning at all the sexual affairs which were part of his weeks in New York. This she would discover later. While he was away from her, he wrote her

Dylan in New York, photographed by Lee Miller
for Vogue

very passionate letters. As always when they were separated, he felt insecure and in need of reassurance. He must have felt disoriented and lonely at times. 'I am no globe-trotter, no cosmopolitan.' He wrote too in the knowledge that he was being unfaithful to her, and alert to the possibility that she was doing the same. In Laugharne, with young children, aged and infirm parents-in-law, very little money, and in the damp Welsh winter, was Caitlin consoled when she read, 'Be good to me as I am good, forever, to you, my love. I love you every second of the day'? A phrase in another letter will have been less easily brushed aside: 'I think of you...waking up alone in our beautiful bedroom–please Christ, my love, it is always alone'. His fears were justified, for she was consoling herself with young men from the town, at first for pleasure, later as much for revenge. He was apprehensive about her – how is she really, he wrote to his parents. He needed her to be there for him.

Caitlin was very suspicious of how Dylan had spent his time in America. She might have worried less had he returned with the money he had gone there to earn, but he had little to show for his time away. (In his absence she had run up debts, including one of £150 with the chemist in Laugharne, who sold groceries and alcohol as well as medicines.) When she was presented with

proof that he had started an affair in New York, she threatened to leave him, and might well have done, had she had somewhere to go. She hated the public Dylan; she had married and devoted herself to the poet, not the actor and 'professional charm boy'. And she was bored in Laugharne, without any real friends, finding solace only in drink. She was trapped in 'this Poet's nest where the poet never is'. Dylan could not ignore her unhappiness and her growing dislike of the place. He too began to think of escape, of leaving behind 'the general hell of sickness, children, excruciating worry, the eternal yellow-grey drizzle...'. To make matters worse, Margaret Taylor had bought herself a holiday cottage in the lower town, close to 'Eros', their first home. Dylan and Caitlin were very happy to be the recipients of her money and kindness, but they did not want to repeat their situation in Oxford where she made herself part of their daily lives.

Margaret Taylor felt strongly that Dylan should not go back to America for another series of readings, and she began to search for somewhere in London where he might live and so be able to find other work. All through the summer of 1951 he was gnawed at by money worries. He wanted to leave Laugharne but could not until he had paid his debts. He could see no way of doing this. He was working slowly, very slowly on his play for voices, at this point called 'Llareggub', although he did manage to raise money on the promise of the finished text. In the early spring he completed two poems, one the comic 'Lament', the other one of his best-known, 'Do not go gentle into that good night', inspired by his father's illness and imminent death. D.J. Thomas had been in his younger days a difficult and an irascible man. Now age and illness had softened him.

Do not go gentle into that good night,
Old age should burn and rave at close of day;
Rage, rage against the dying of the light.

In August 1951, while still in Laugharne, Dylan finished what was to be his last poem, 'Poem on his Birthday', first begun some two years earlier. He wrote looking out at the estuary and the river, seeing in the birds and the fish the movement of all living things towards death.

In the mustardseed sun,
By full tilt river and switchback sea
Where cormorants scud,
In his house on stilts high among beaks
And palavers of birds
This sandgrain day in the bent bay's grave
He celebrates and spurns
His driftwood thirty-fifth windturned age;
Herons spire and spear.

Laugharne, September 1953: Dylan stands with his first son Llewelyn behind Aeronwy, his mother, Colm and Caitlin.

Shortly afterwards he and his family moved into Margaret Taylor's latest home for them, the basement flat of 54 Delancey Street in Camden Town, north London. Once again, Dylan was full of good intentions – for BBC work, for new poems and stories – but nothing came of them. If Margaret Taylor thought she might prevent his escaping again to America, she was to be disappointed. Once it was agreed that Caitlin could accompany him, she dropped her opposition to the plan and, leaving Llewelyn and Aeronwy in school and Colm with a young woman in Laugharne, she set off with Dylan across the Atlantic in January 1952. They were to stay until mid-May: four months of travelling, drinking, disagreement and anger. Caitlin's presence did nothing to protect Dylan from the demons inside or outside him. She had no role, there was nothing useful for her to do. She could only look on as he held centre stage. She did not ensure that he brought money home with him, for she felt that she was owed a good time. They returned to Laugharne no better off, indeed in a worse position than before, for now the Inland Revenue and National Insurance officials were on Dylan's trail.

Bronchitis, pleurisy, money worries all but overwhelmed him, making it impossible for him to fulfil his commitment to the BBC (waiting for *Under Milk Wood*) and to his editor at his publishers J.M. Dent, who wanted to consolidate his reputation with the publication of his collected poems. Dent had already been waiting for several months for his preface to the volume, for Dylan had decided against a conventional preface in prose, choosing instead to produce a prologue in verse. 'The first and last lines of the poem rhyme,' he explained; 'the second and the last but one; & so on & so on. Why I acrosticked myself like this, don't ask me.' Whether by design or by chance, such a difficult and demanding task left him no time or opportunity for writing anything else.

Collected Poems 1934–52 finally appeared in November 1952 and was very well received. Cyril Connolly wrote that, at his best, Dylan Thomas was unique; Philip Toynbee called him the greatest living poet in English. The book sold well on both sides of the Atlantic, and won Dylan £250 and the Foyle's Poetry Prize for 1952. It is unlikely that this success brought him very much pleasure. Inside he was full of doubts and fears. A few weeks after publication, his father died, blind and in pain. His mother too was unwell, although she would recover and outlive her son by five years. His sister, Nancy, had developed cancer and had been operated on earlier in 1952. (She was to die the following spring, a few months before him.) Caitlin was pregnant and insisted on

Dylan in his writing shed in the summer of 1953, deeply troubled and writing very little

having an abortion, which left her feeling weak and low. Dylan could not be certain that the child would have been his. Money was still a worry, even though his book was selling well and the recordings of his readings which he had made in the USA were beginning to bring in revenue. Margaret Taylor was threatening to sell the Boat House; it was costing her more than she could now afford. Another new benefactor, Marged Howard-Stepney, promised to step in and take over, but she died suddenly before this could be arranged.

Worst of all, Dylan was not writing. He read, talked, performed, lectured, did anything and everything but write. Caitlin accused him of giving up, of opting out. He knew otherwise.

For a whole year I have been able to write nothing, nothing, nothing at all but one tangled, sentimental poem as preface to a collection of poems written years ago. Perhaps it doesn't seem and sound – that phrase 'I have been able to write nothing' – the throttling bloody hell it's been to me for this whole waste of a twisted year...I went on all over the States, ranting poems to enthusiastic audiences...and gradually I began to feel nervous about the job in front of me, the job of writing, making things in words, by myself, again. The

more I used words, the more frightened I became of using them in my own work once more. ...I came home fearful and jangled. There was my hut on a cliff, full of pencil and paper, things to stare at, room to breathe and feel and think. But I couldn't write a word. I tried then to write a poem, dreading it beforehand, a few obscure lines every dumb day, and the printed result shook and battered me in any faith in myself and workman's pride left to me. I couldn't write a word after that.

In April 1953, with fewer and fewer options left to him, Dylan set out for a third time for America, very much against the wishes of his newly widowed mother and of his wife, who accused him of going in search of 'flattery, idleness and infidelity'. This tour was a more placid affair, and lasted only six weeks. He had agreed to give a solo reading of *Under Milk Wood* at Harvard, but the play was not finished, so that he was writing new material right up to the last moment. This first reading was a success; *Under Milk Wood* was to bring him the adulation Caitlin feared and despised. The infidelity also, for he had begun an affair with Liz Reitell, John Brinnin's assistant at the Poetry Center. She was arranging a stage production, with a cast of actors, for which Dylan had eleven days to prepare the script. Last-minute passages were typed up and delivered to the cast less than an hour before the performance.

Dylan never completely finished *Under Milk Wood*. None the less, it is his best-known and best-loved work, eclipsing in fame and popularity his greatest poems and his prose writings. The idea for his 'play for voices' had grown within him over many years. He had first talked to Bert Trick in 1932 about writing a Welsh equivalent of James Joyce's *Ulysses*, a portrait of a town over a 24-hour span. Ultimately his aim was more modest. In 1939, after he and Caitlin had taken part in local theatricals organized by Richard and Frances Hughes, Dylan remarked that what Laugharne needed was a play about the town, with well-known characters playing themselves, but it would be some time before the play as we know it began to take recognizable shape. Essential to it was Dylan's direct experience of life in New Quay and Laugharne, and his compassionate observation and gentle satirizing of his own childhood past in his stories and radio broadcasts. The shape of New Quay on the edge of Cardigan Bay; the combination of eccentricity and idyll which Laugharne offered; the hours spent in Brown's Hotel listening to the gossip of the town – these he combined with the skills he had gained through writing film scripts in the 1940s. In

Under Milk Wood, his 'comedy of humours' (Kenneth Tynan), his 'uproarious and singing lament' (Raymond Williams), Dylan made his peace with Wales, he declared a truce. It is unlikely that this would have been permanent had he lived longer and rediscovered his powers as a writer. He knew the play's worth. He knew full well that there were more difficult and revealing worlds to explore, for which he seemed no longer to have the skill or the strength.

He continued to work on *Under Milk Wood* during the summer of 1953 in Laugharne, but to little effect. In July, with Caitlin and Aeronwy, he visited the International Eisteddfod at Llangollen – the furthest north he had ever travelled in Wales – and wrote an affectionate account of it for a BBC radio broadcast. Otherwise he did very little writing other than draft and redraft letters and fragments of verse, weaving and spinning words and phrases web-like around him. It is easy to see now that he was in very deep trouble, that he had reached a point where no one could help him. He had long managed to keep reality at arm's length; now it seems that he had lost touch with it completely. His solution was to escape once again to New York. Before he left, he spent a day with the photographer Rollie McKenna visiting some of the places and people who had meant most to him. He recorded a brief

The River Taf from Llanybri – where 'haystacked/Hollow farms in a Throng/Of water cluck and cling'

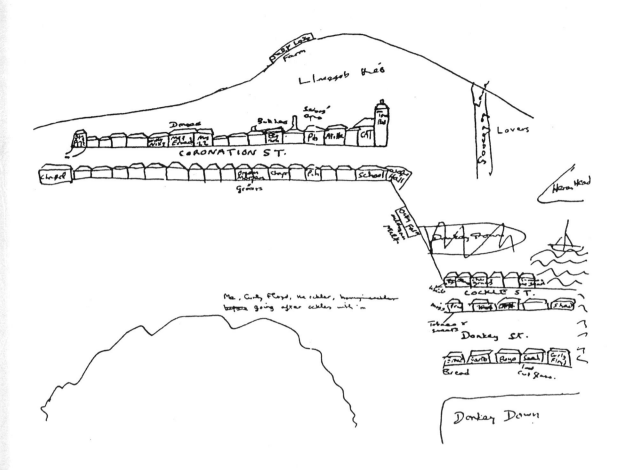

ABOVE *Dylan's sketch of Llareggub. The position of the town under Llareg-gub Hill recalls Laugharne; the harbour is reminiscent of New Quay.*

LEFT *Dylan's writing shed, his 'seashaken house/On a breakneck of rocks/Tangled with chirrup and fruit'*

contribution to a radio programme on Laugharne; when he visited his mother for the last time to say good-bye, he went back three times to kiss her. Caitlin spent a few days with him in London; there, at last, he delivered his script of *Under Milk Wood* to the BBC and was given copies to take with him to New York. He left England for America on October 19; twenty-one days later he was dead.

EPILOGUE

It is said that shortly before he died Dylan Thomas opened his eyes and said calmly, 'Tonight in my home the men have their arms around one another, and they are singing.' So many stories cluster around his death and burial that it is tempting to dismiss these last words as more wished for than real. Yet in his final hours, knowing that he was close to death, his senses already beginning to float free, it is possible that he was visited by a memory of Wales, by an image of men, together in a safe place. For the greater part of his life he felt an outsider, that he never completely belonged. Home, he discovered, could only be 'a resting place between places'. Happily, in his writing he managed to achieve the fusion which eluded him in his own life.

Dylan often told his friends that he would not live into old age. None the less, his death on 9 November 1953, only two weeks after his thirty-ninth birthday, came as a great shock. It also affected many people on both sides of the Atlantic who had never met him, who knew him only through his writing or by reputation. At once he became the stuff of legend. Social rebel, *poète maudit*, Wales's greatest son – he entered the world of myth and iconography.

Caitlin brought his body from New York back home to Laugharne. He was taken to the Pelican, his mother's house in the main street. The Boat House, perched on the edge of the estuary, would have posed problems for a coffin and its bearers. On 24 November he was buried in the churchyard of St Martin's, the parish church of Laugharne. Many stories are told of his funeral – of the cock that crowed just as the coffin entered the churchyard, of how the poet Louis MacNeice accidentally dropped sandwiches

Dylan in the church cemetery, Laugharne, November 1949, 'inside the railings of a tomb, my hair uncut for months...blown up like a great, dancing, mousey busby'

The new churchyard, St Martin's church, Laugharne, where Dylan was buried on 24 November 1953.

instead of flowers on to the grave. The mourners were many and various: friends from London, Dylan's 'Swansea gang', local neighbours and friends. The pubs stayed open until late in the night. The mood was more that of a wake than of a traditional burial; pain and regret found expression in ebullience and farce.

Caitlin felt doubly aggrieved, resentful that Dylan had made his escape, leaving her with children, debts and no apparent future, and mourning the loss of the man in whom she had invested much. She had three young children, a house she did not own and a backlog of debts. In fact, her situation was less precarious than she thought. Soon Dylan Thomas's estate would begin to earn sums of money which far exceeded everyone's expectations. Yet at the time of his death he had felt only failure. He did not like what he had become: he preferred the young man he once was. 'Then I was arrogant and lost. Now I am humble and found. I prefer that other.'

This is not at all how he is perceived today. Almost half a century after his death, Dylan Thomas is the soaring, lyrical voice of Wales, her most famous writer and son. From the outset his poetry was romantic, incantatory and rhythmical, visionary in its responses, in harmony with that of other Welsh writers before him, quite unlike the intellectual, politically engaged verse of his own

Dylan's work table in his writing shed, 'his slant, racking house/And the hewn coils of his trade'

A wooden cross marks Dylan's grave in the new churchyard of St Martin's church, Laugharne. Caitlin was buried with him in August 1994.

contemporaries, Eliot, Auden, Spender and Empson. His idea of the poet – seer and bard – was also closer to the Welsh rather than English traditions. But he was also drawn to and manipulated the character of the *poète maudit*, and it is in this guise that he most holds our attention – the martyr-poet, the man who soared too high and paid the price, who descended into his own particular hell, his bardic robes clutched round him.

Because he drew so powerfully on the places he knew, using them as the bedrock of his poetry, Dylan Thomas's Wales has now a certain legendary quality. Even though his relationship with the country of his birth was never an easy one, he tacitly acknowledged that Wales was the prism through which he saw the world.

> I hear the bouncing hills
> Grow larked and greener at berry brown
>   Fall and the dew larks sing
> Taller this thunderclap spring, and how
>   More spanned with angels ride
> The mansouled fiery islands! Oh,
>   Holier then their eyes,
> And my shining men no more alone
>   As I sail out to die.

CHRONOLOGY OF DYLAN THOMAS'S LIFE

27 October 1914 Dylan Marlais Thomas born at 5 Cwmdonkin Drive, Uplands, Swansea, son of D.J. Thomas and his wife Florence.

September 1925 Goes to Swansea Grammar School where his father is Senior English Master and he becomes friends with Dan Jones.

February 1927 Poem 'The Second Best' published in the *Boy's Own Paper*.

April 1930 Begins the first of the notebooks into which he copies his early poems. He continues doing this until 1934.

July 1931 Leaves school, aged 16, with very few obvious qualifications. Goes to work as a reporter on the *South Wales Daily Post*.

Autumn 1932 Joins the Swansea Little Theatre.

December 1932 Stops working as a journalist and begins his life as a full-time writer.

February 1933 Death of his aunt Ann Jones of Fernhill. Writes poem 'After the Funeral'.

March 1933 'And death shall have no dominion' published in the *New English Weekly*, first poem published in a London magazine.

August 1933 First visit to London – to stay with his sister, Nancy, and her husband.

September 1933 Poem published in the 'Poet's Corner' of the *Sunday Referee* – 'That sanity be kept' – leads to correspondence with Pamela Hansford Johnson.
D.J. Thomas has treatment for cancer of the tongue.

February 1934 In London, meets Pamela Hansford Johnson for the first time.

April 1934 Wins the *Sunday Referee*'s Book Prize which guarantees the publication of his first book. Several magazines now publishing his poems.

May 1934 Spends the Whitsun weekend with his new friend Glyn Jones in west Wales, visiting Llanstephan and Laugharne.

July 1934 Goes with Bert Trick to hear Oswald Mosley speak at a fascist rally in Swansea.

September 1934 Pamela Hansford Johnson and her mother come to Swansea.

November 1934 Moves to London, to 5 Redcliffe Gardens, Fulham, with Alfred Janes and Mervyn Levy.

December 1934 First book, *18 Poems*, published.

February 1935 Letter from Vernon Watkins begins a very important friendship.

April 1935 Visits Richard Hughes at the Castle House, Laugharne. Spends several weeks with historian A.J.P. Taylor and his wife Margaret in their Derbyshire cottage.

July 1935 In Ireland for several weeks, in a very isolated house in west Donegal with poet Geoffrey Grigson.

April 1936 Meets Caitlin Macnamara in the Wheatsheaf pub; spends several days with her before going to Cornwall.

July 1936 To Fishguard with Alfred Janes, by way of Laugharne. Return journey with Augustus John and Caitlin ends in argument with John.

September 1936 Second book, *25 Poems*, published by J.M. Dent.

December 1936 D.J. Thomas retires from teaching. Soon he will sell 5 Cwmdonkin Drive and move with his wife to Bishopston.

April 1937 First radio broadcast – 'Life and the Modern Poet', for BBC Welsh service.

May 1937 With Caitlin to Cornwall.

11 July 1937 Dylan and Caitlin marry at Penzance register office. Afterwards they stay with Dylan's parents at Bishopston, then at Caitlin's mother's house in Hampshire.

May 1938 They move into their first home in Laugharne – 'Eros' in Gosport Street.

August 1938 Move to 'Sea View', a larger house higher up the town.

30 January 1939 First child, Llewelyn, born in Hampshire.

August 1939 Third book, *The Map of Love*, published.

December 1939 *The World I Breathe*, a selection of poems and short stories, published in the USA, Dylan's first appearance there.

April 1940 *Portrait of the Artist as a Young Dog*, story collection, published by J.M. Dent.

May 1940 Fails army medical and so escapes active service in World War II. Leaves Laugharne to escape creditors. Spends time with his parents at Bishopston and with friends in Wiltshire. Moves between Bishopston and London in search of work.

February 1941 German bombs destroy the centre of Swansea.

April 1941 Dylan sells his early notebooks through book dealer Bertram Rota.

May 1941 Dylan and family stay with Frances Hughes in the Castle House, Laugharne.

September 1941 Dylan begins to work as a script writer for the Strand Film Company.

Summer 1942 Caitlin spends much of her time at Talsarn, Cardiganshire, Dylan visiting her from London.

Autumn 1942 Brings Caitlin to live in London, in Manresa Road, Chelsea.

3 March 1943 Daughter Aeronwy born. Dylan now broadcasting regularly for the BBC.

April 1944 To avoid air raids in London, moves to Bosham, near Chichester.

July 1944 Returns to Wales, to Llangain, near Carmarthen, to live with his parents in their cottage at Blaen Cwm.

September 1944 Beginning of productive months spent in 'Majoda', a rented bungalow in New Quay.

October 1944 Having agreed to be Vernon Watkins's best man, Dylan fails to show up at his wedding.

Summer 1945 Leave New Quay after shooting incident. Dylan and family move between Llangain, London and, finally, Oxford where they are lent a summer-house on the banks of the River Cherwell by Alan and Margaret Taylor.

February 1946 Publication of *Deaths and Entrances*.

April 1947 In Italy (in Rapallo, Florence and Elba), paid for by a travel grant from the Society of Authors.

September 1947 Moves to the Manor House, South Leigh, Oxfordshire, again thanks to Margaret Taylor. Dylan works in London on filmscripts and for the BBC.

October 1948 Margaret Taylor buys the Boat House in Laugharne.

March 1949 Visits Prague as a guest of the Czech government.

May 1949 Moves once again to Laugharne, to the Boat House, his last home. Approached by John Brinnin and invited to visit America to give poetry readings.

24 July 1949 Second son and third child, Colm, born.

February–June 1950 First American tour.

January 1951 To Iran, to write a filmscript for the Anglo-Iranian Oil Company.

Summer 1951 Working on his last poems and on *Under Milk Wood*.

September 1951 Moves to basement flat in Delancey Street, Camden Town, London, found for him by Margaret Taylor so that he would be more easily able to get work.

January–May 1952 Second American visit, this time accompanied by Caitlin.

November 1952 *Collected Poems 1934–52* published.

16 December 1952 Death of D.J. Thomas, aged seventy-six.

April–June 1953 Third American tour. Dylan's sister Nancy dies in Bombay of cancer.

May 1953 Performs *Under Milk Wood* for the first time, in New York.

July 1953 Visits International Eisteddfod at Llangollen in north Wales with Caitlin and Aeronwy.

9 October 1953 Leaves Laugharne for London to begin his fourth American tour.

5 November 1953 Collapses at his hotel in New York and is taken to St Vincent's Hospital. Caitlin arrives in New York to find him in a coma.

9 November 1953 Dies in New York.

24 November 1953 Dylan Thomas buried in the graveyard of St Martin's church, Laugharne.

INDEX

ACKNOWLEDGEMENTS

A book such as this cannot be written without the help and scholarship of other writers and commentators on Dylan Thomas. I am happy to acknowledge my debt to John Ackerman, James A. Davies, Walford Davies, Paul Ferris, Ralph Maud, Aerony Thomas, Caitlin Thomas and George Tremlett. I would also like to thank Jeff Towns for his very generous help. I am grateful to the publishers J.M. Dent and to the Trustees for the Copyrights of Dylan Thomas for permission to quote from Dylan Thomas's published works.

Endpapers: Swansea, seen from Mumbles; Half Title: The Taf Estuary and the Boat House, Laugharne; Page 2: Dylan's writing shed near the Boat House, Laugharne.

First published in Great Britain in 1999 by Weidenfeld & Nicolson
Text copyright © Hilary Laurie, 1999
The moral right of Hilary Laurie to be identified as the author of this work has been asserted in accordance with the Copyright, Designs and Patents Act of 1988
Design and layout copyright © Weidenfeld & Nicolson, 1999

A CIP catalogue record for this book is available from the British Library
ISBN 0 297 82481 3

Picture research: Elizabeth Lowing/Jeff Towns
Edited by: Anthony Lambert
Designed by: Staziker Jones
Set in: Stone Serif

All photographs © Kathy de Witt, excluding: p.7 Nora Summers/Jeff Towns/Dylans Bookstore Collection (JT/DBC); p.12 unknown; p.13 Paul Ferris; p.16 JT/DBC; p.17 Christina Gascoigne; p.18 JT/DBC; p.26 *South Wales Evening Post*, Swansea; p. 27, 38, 48 JT/DBC; p.50 unknown; p.58 Alfred Janes/National Museum and Galleries of Wales, Cardiff; p.60 Paul Ferris; p.61 unknown; p.62 Lady Avebury; p.66, 68 Nora Summers/JT/DBC; p.73 JT/DBC; p.79 Nora Summers; p.80. 83 Vernon Watkins/JT/DBC; p.87 Rollie McKenna; p.90 unknown; p.91 Nora Summers; p.92 JT/DBC; p.97 unknown; p.100 John Deakin/*Vogue*/Conde Nast; p.101 Nora Summers; p.104 Rupert Shephard/National Portrait Gallery; p.111 Douglas Glass; p.112 Hulton Picture Library; p.120 Rollie McKenna; p.123, 126 JT/DBC; p.134 Rollie McKenna; p.136 JT/DBC; p.139 Lee Miller/Lee Miller Archive; p.141, 142, 144 Rollie McKenna; p.149 unknown; p.150 John Deakin/*Vogue*/Conde Nast; p.154 Vincent A Lloyd/JT/DBC.

Weidenfeld & Nicolson
The Orion Publishing Group Ltd
5 Upper Saint Martin's Lane
London WC2H 9EA
Printed and bound in France by *Partenaires-Livres*®